OUT OF THE DARKNESS AND INTO THE BLUE

Surprising Secrets, Tactics, and Training Concepts:
A Memoir from one of Kalamazoo's Top Cops

ROBERT T. CHRISTENSEN

ISBN: 1495301052
ISBN 13: 9781495301056
Library of Congress Control Number: 2014901520
CreateSpace Independent Publishing Platform
North Charleston, South Carolina

DEDICATION

To my mom, dad, and sisters, whom I protected by never telling you what I really did at work. I feel as though you never knew what I did over twenty-five years of my life. However, it was my intent to have you not worry about me. I did not want you to live your lives wondering if I was going to come home or not.

ACKNOWLEDGEMENTS

My career priority was to serve and protect the city of Kalamazoo. I am forever grateful to the citizens of Kalamazoo, my coworkers at Kalamazoo Public Safety, the criminal justice professionals throughout the judicial system, the local government officials, both past and present, and the neighborhood volunteers. I am confident that through your continued efforts, the city of Kalamazoo will always be one of the best communities in our nation. It was an honor to serve you all.

IN MEMORY OF

Officer Eric Zapata, Kalamazoo Public Safety
End of Watch—April 18, 2011

Officer Scot Beyerstedt, Mattawan Police Department
End of Watch—July 26, 2005

Officer Owen Fisher, Flint Police Department
End of Watch—July 16, 2005

Never a day goes by that I don't think about my brothers.

IN HONOR OF

The 4,235 police officers who died in the line of duty during my career.

1988–2012

You will never be forgotten.

TABLE OF CONTENTS

"If you do this job properly, there is nothing more noble you will do with your life."

Dan Weston, Chief,
Kalamazoo Department of Public Safety

INTRODUCTION

Throughout my public safety career, I often thought about documenting my experiences as a police officer. My intention was not to write a book but to simply try to remember everything I had experienced, so that one day, in my older years, I would not forget all that I'd lived through. As I began documenting my experiences, I soon realized that they were nothing new but certainly noteworthy. Perhaps other officers, and even those aspiring to become police officers, could benefit from my experiences, actions, and outcomes to improve their own investigatory techniques. My stories could help them formulate their own decisions related to what I had experienced or even save an officer's life.

I also want to inspire each individual in our society to realize that, regardless of your race, color, religion, national origin, age, sex, or sexual orientation, the only things stopping you from attaining your dreams and goals in life are the obstacles that you build yourself. Never think that you can't do something just because of who you are.

This book is not your typical memoir, I should add. Throughout the book I insert tactics, training concepts, and suggestions to help the reader understand what being a cop is really all about. Also, for my colleagues, I try to instill a sense of renewed professionalism to help bring them back to the attitude they had when they graduated from the academy: that of truly *wanting to help people.*

Out of the Darkness and into the Blue is not an instructional guide or textbook. It is a book written from my personal viewpoint and based on my observations, feelings, and experiences. The facts and circumstances depicted are what I, but nobody else, experienced. The book is not meant to express my opinion or explain the legal aspects of any given situation. I simply want each reader to experience what it was like to be in the patrol car of Public Safety Officer Robert Todd Christensen.

My goals in writing this book are as diverse as the book itself. First, as a police trainer, I realize that this book could make a huge impact at three points during an officer's career:

1) A police cadet in academy training and during college coursework.
2) A newly hired rookie officer.
3) Officers at any point in their law enforcement careers.

Second, I want to effectively convey to the general public what goes through the mind of a police officer, how our professional experiences as officers affect and guide our daily habits and routines when dealing with the public, and how those experiences affect our personal lives both on and off duty.

Finally, I want my experiences to serve as moments of inspiration to other criminal justice professionals who, at some point in their careers, will need to find that inner fire of self-improvement in order to stay motivated to do their very best at all times. The last day of a career should be just as exciting as the first!

As officers, we're often referred to as creatures of habit. One great habit that I have developed throughout my police and military careers is to learn by others' mistakes. Unfortunately, this lesson is often the result of an officer's injury or death. In the end, though, we should all ask ourselves this question: "What would I have done?" This is something I asked myself daily. Police officers make the best Monday morning quarterbacks, and we're quick to second-guess not only ourselves, but also our partners. We are also masters of learning from tragedy, especially when that tragedy happens to us! We learn best by doing and that in turn builds on our training and experience.

In *Out of the Darkness and into the Blue*, it is my intent to insist that officers continue to ask themselves that question as they read through each of my experiences: "What would I have done?"

I have tried to recreate events, locales, and conversations from my memories of them. In order to maintain their anonymity, in some instances I have changed the names of individuals and places. Also, I may have changed some identifying characteristics and details, such as physical properties, occupations, and places of residence.

NEVER QUIT—ALWAYS FIGHT

My career began on May 27, 1988, in the small town of Lawrence, Michigan. The department consisted of a chief of police and two patrol officers. The officers shared one cruiser (a used 1986 Chevrolet Impala) to patrol a town of approximately one thousand residents. Up until March 4, 1990, my newly found career was filled with constant learning events and a complete lack of training or mentoring to prepare me for the toxic, corrosive, and violent nature of my chosen career. Within my first two years as a rookie cop in a small town, I had already begun to develop bad habits and a routine of complacency in my patrol tactics.

On March 4, 1990, at 12:20 a.m., my career nearly came to an end. It started out like any typical midnight shift in southwest Michigan. The damp night air was a comfortable forty degrees, hinting that spring was just around the corner. The warmer air created a heavy blanket of fog that hovered over the slushy, snow-covered ground. Just twenty minutes into my shift, I found myself in a life-and-death situation for which I was totally unprepared.

The shift started out routinely as I drove my patrol car onto the main north/south road in the village. Perhaps it was fate that inserted itself into my life, for I took a different route than usual out of the department's single-car garage. Instead of turning left out of the garage, like I normally did, I turned right.

After I passed through the only traffic signal in town, I spotted an inbound vehicle moving fast. The dash radar let out a high-pitch tone that coincided with the speed of forty-eight in the thirty-five–mile-per-hour zone. My first traffic stop of the night was fast approaching me. However, little did I know that in just a few moments, I would be in a fight for my life that was nearly a career-ending tragedy.

I spun around on the suspect vehicle as it drove past and followed it only a few short blocks to where it turned abruptly into a driveway of the suspect driver's home. At that point, I made a sequence of safety mistakes that would lead to an ass kicking and what could have been my untimely death.

I didn't call out my traffic stop on the radio; nobody knew where I was or the peril I would soon be in. The driver, Juan Rico, was the lone occupant of the car. He immediately jumped out after he pulled into his driveway. My cruiser was directly behind his car, spotlight shining through the back window, emergency lights flashing. It seemed as if we both jumped out of our cars at the same time as I yelled out to him, "Sir, have a seat back in your car!" He yelled, "Fuck you!" and motioned with his hand for me to go away.

Rico turned around and began to walk toward the front door of his house, only a few yards away. I followed him to the front steps and told him I needed to see his driver's license. He gestured again, motioning with his hand behind his back for me to go away. I knew I wasn't going to let him enter his home, and I was hell bent on arresting him for failing to display his driver's license.

I could feel the adrenaline rushing through my body with my every step. My heart was pounding, and tunnel vision intensified. I focused only on Rico's left wrist. As soon as he stepped up on the three small steps to his home, I grabbed onto his left wrist in an effort to stop him from going inside. The next thing I remember seeing was a flash of light, and I felt a shock to my face that knocked me backward. Was I just shot in the face or punched? I had no clue.

Rico had his arm wrapped around my neck in a choke hold and was punching me repeatedly in the face. I was trapped in his arm with a strangling headlock around my neck. I was just trying to breathe! My efforts to strike back were totally ineffective as he kept punching me and punching me in the face. After multiple strikes to my face, I remember telling myself that it didn't even hurt anymore, because my face was so numb and cold from the blood and pain.

The blood gushing from my nose is what saved my life at that moment. It caused my head to slip out of Rico's grasp. As I squirmed my head out of his hold and got back onto my feet, I stumbled backward away from him. I was just trying to get away. Everything seemed to be in slow motion, and I was in shock from what had just happened. Knowing I needed help, I pulled out the portable radio on my gun belt (with no shoulder microphone attached) and screamed for help: "County three-two-two, I need backup!"

I was stumbling backward as Rico charged after me and attacked again, this time pushing me backward at my chest and pinning me against the hood of the patrol car. He was punching me in the chest, neck, and face. He was a punching, screaming mad man. I rolled away to my right side and landed on the ground on my right hip. I remember telling myself, "Get up and fight, god dammit; fight this mother fucker!" All the while, I was hoping I could last long enough for backup officers to arrive. As I stood up on my feet, Rico was about ten feet away from me, still at the front of my cruiser. He seemed to be out of breath also and was bent over leaning on his knees with his hands. That's when I thought to myself, "He's too strong, and he's going to kill me if he gets hold of me again."

I remember feeling weak and staggering on my feet. I was out of breath with fingers frozen from the snow and lack of circulation. Wiping the blood out of my eyes, I couldn't feel my face, but I could feel pieces of broken teeth in my mouth. My tongue was split open, and my whole body felt numb. I could hardly breathe, and the air seemed to burn with every breath I took. I could barely stay on my feet. Dazed, confused, and covered in blood, I had no strength.

I thought to myself, "I'm going to have to shoot this guy." In that same moment, I pictured what the headlines of the local paper would read: "Lawrence Police Officer Guns down Unarmed Mexican." Later I found out that this was the worst possible thought I could have ever imagined. The thought of legal ramifications or liability in a life and death struggle should never have entered my mind. Nonetheless, it did, and I blame these self-destructive thoughts on my lack of realistic, scenario-based training. To this day, I regret not shooting him.

The thought of shooting Rico immediately vanished, and I ran toward him, not even knowing what I was going to do. I grabbed him around the back of the head and delivered the knee strike of a lifetime to his face, which knocked him out cold. I was shocked that what I did actually worked! That was my chance to get the cuffs on this fucker. I finally had control. Time sped up again. I was finally on the attack.

I remember handcuffing Rico and then being hit on the back of the head by some object, but I had no idea what. It turned out that Rico's wife had come running outside and hit me with a broom handle. I pushed her down into the snow and found my radio next to me. I yelled into the radio again. "County three-two-two, I need an ambulance…for me!" I passed out on top of a still unconscious Rico at the back door of my cruiser.

I could hear the sirens wailing in the distance, but it felt like the sound was in a dream. Then I remember being moved, with hands all over me. I could tell I was being back boarded, and I recognized the voices. Lawrence quick response team member Rick Leonard kept telling me, "Todd, you're gonna be OK. Just relax. You got him. You got him."

I woke up staring at the bright lights in the ceiling of the ambulance and looked over to Paramedic Jim Nelson. I remember telling him, "Fuck this shit. I'm quitting. For eight thirty-two an hour, fuck this shit."

Jim leaned over me and said, "Todd, you can't quit. You're a cop. This is what you know, man."

I just lay there silent, thinking of my life and how I had fucked up. Still, I agreed with Jim. I glanced over at him. "You're right. I'm a cop. I can't quit." I asked him to unstrap my left arm so I could pick my nose. God, the dried up blood in my nose was bothering me so bad. This brief, but meaningful conversation changed my life forever. I will never quit!

I ended up being treated and released from the hospital that same night. I had a broken nose and a fractured right little finger, and I required stitches to my right knee from the knee strike that saved my life that night. I was alive, and I thanked God for it.

Rico was also treated and released from the hospital, and then arrested for driving while intoxicated and resisting/obstructing police. His blood alcohol content was .17 percent. He spent just one night in jail and served out the remainder of his time on probation. The county prosecutor told me that, based on the totality of circumstances, I would have been justified in using deadly force during this assault.

The suspect admitted to consuming a twelve-pack of beer and had no idea that he had been stopped by the police. During the interview of Juan Rico at the hospital, he stated: "When I got home, I just got out of my car and started walking toward the house when the officer came up behind me, jumped on my back, and started hitting me. I had no choice but to hit him back."

Before this incident took place, I'd been having a recurring dream that, when I was in a fight, my punches never worked. Actually, they were nightmares of what would happen to me. After this incident, the dreams never came back to me. I believe it was a lack of realistic training at the police academy that failed to prepare me for a real fight. I had no idea what it felt like to get punched, choked out, or have a ground fight with an actively aggressive subject. A new cop's first fight should never be like mine.

This incident taught me many things. Most importantly, though, I promised myself that from then on, I would always throw the first punch and be the aggressor in any fight, not a victim. I could have been killed on March 4, 1990, but I wasn't. It was a hard lesson I had to learn through blood and tears. I returned to work three days later with two black eyes and a broken nose. Going back on patrol was the best thing for me. I needed to get back in the game and regain my confidence.

PREPARE YOURSELF TO WIN THE FIGHT

This event involved a series of tactical blunders, and I was doomed from the moment I started my shift. I beg you, please learn from my mistakes.

- Do not wear a jacket while on patrol. A jacket will constrict your movements during a physical confrontation. Instead, under your bullet-resistant vest, wear cold weather gear that's light weight and made of a product that wicks away moisture and keeps you warm in a cold environment.

- Call out every traffic stop to dispatch. Every time!
- Carry all intermediate weapons—pepper spray, impact weapons, Taser.
- Wear a shoulder or collar radio mic attached to your portable radio.
- Wear footwear made from lightweight and comfortable material that keeps your feet warm in the winter and cool in the summer. I prefer a lightweight, waterproof tactical boot in the winter and black running shoes in the summer (to allow more running speed during foot pursuits). Heavy clumsy boots are no match for suspects in gym shoes.
- Attend quality subject control training sessions that include scenario-based training modules in a realistic setting and that allow you to experience physical exertion during full-force, physical confrontations, ground fighting, and physical exhaustion.
- Practice changing and evolving scenarios relative to deadly force during realistic training, and have a complete understanding and working knowledge of the force continuum.
- Write the use-of-force reports with descriptive detail. Do not generalize, but paint a clear picture in the mind of the reader that explains the subject's actions and the officer's response during use-of-force situations.
- Continue to hone your skills throughout your career. Subject control techniques are all perishable skills. Every officer must *never stop learning.*

- Maintain a high level of physical fitness and wellness. Cardiovascular stamina, absolute strength, proper diet and nutrition, and a warrior mind-set with a never-quit attitude must be paramount. Do not waiver at any time during your entire career. You never know when you'll be in a fight for your life. Mentally prepare yourself to win each and every confrontation. Being aggressively assaulted is not a matter of *if*, but *when* it will happen to you.

It would be only two weeks after this incident that I would face a similar situation, but this time the outcome was much different. I learned from the mistakes of my first attack and gained the confidence I needed in this second event to help me realize that I can win in any confrontation. Through mental planning, training, and possessing a never-quit attitude and a winning mind-set, officers can prepare themselves to gain the tactical edge needed in physical confrontations.

I was dispatched in answer to a report of an escaped felon from Jackson Prison who was hiding in his mother's apartment. The mother had called police without her son knowing. This time I was able to plan out my actions, and I remember telling myself, "I'm going to get this guy." I called for backup immediately, parked my patrol car out of sight behind the apartment complex, and made my approach on foot undetected.

My backup officer was a solid five miles away, but I knew that help was on the way. I still felt obligated to make contact before backup arrived, a tactic I would not recommend unless you're compromised and must initiate contact. I knocked on the door of the apartment. There was no answer. I knocked again, and the door was opened only a crack by an obviously scared elderly woman, the mother. In this split second it was as if we read each other's minds. When her eyes shifted to the left of the door, it was like she was saying, "He's behind the door!"

I pushed open the door, but it stopped halfway to the wall because of the suspect hiding behind it. He slammed the door back in my face and jumped out the first floor window. I slammed back, burst into the apartment and jumped out the same window as the suspect. I spotted him running around the back of the building.

I was in foot pursuit and gaining on him fast. I leaped in the air, grabbed onto his head, and pulled him to the ground. The tackle felt great! Right when we hit the ground, I started to punch his head and face repeatedly while I was on his back. He tried to rise up and push me off. He was still resisting arrest! However, his efforts to escape stopped after just two or three punches. (I'll call this taking the wind out of his sails.)

I grabbed onto his arms and handcuffed him just as another police officer ran up behind me. I got him. I won! This was the win I needed to regain the confidence in myself as a cop. It was at this moment in my career that I felt I was reborn. I was officially back in the game.

I learned another amazing tactic from this incident that stayed with me my entire career. The phrase "change their channel to the Law Enforcement Network" was my mantra. I learned that once you decide to go hands-on with a suspect, you must be 100 percent committed to victory and more willing to take them to jail than they are to escape. Also, violence in action is paramount to end a physical confrontation as quickly as possible. Don't allow the suspect an opportunity to fight back or assault you. Your goal should be to end any fight and have control in less than thirty seconds.

You must feel the momentum building, your heart racing, and your adrenaline pumping, to bring all you have to bear on the suspect at that crucial moment of truth. Be offensive, not defensive. I'm a firm believer in offensive tactics, not what is termed "defensive tactics." The mental will to fight, win, and survive must be harnessed and experience in training at the academy level to establish a solid foundation from which to grow and professionalize when honing your subject-control skills. Fortunately, I survived this moment in my career, and it became a platform from which my next twenty-three years would prove to be successful and victorious.

The incident with Juan Rico was not my first physical confrontation with resistive or assaultive suspects. As I look back, I remember that it was actually a series of failed events that led up to this moment in time. The attending factor was my lack of training, not necessarily experience, in dealing with resistive/assaultive subjects. I think I was just lucky up to that point.

Hospital photo after being assaulted by Juan Rico

I WAS LUCKY TO MAKE IT OUT OF MY ROOKIE YEARS ALIVE!

My first shift was on the same night that I graduated from the academy. There was no field training program to speak of, but I already knew the department's standard operating procedures from serving as a reserve police officer for one year before the academy.

The first night on patrol was uneventful, but an exciting moment for me, since I was out on my own, "serving and protecting." Looking back, what I lacked, though, were the communication skills needed to speak to people in an effective and productive manner that was not demeaning but professional. Additionally, I looked very young. I was only nineteen years old, so I not only looked like a super rookie cop, but I also lacked the effective communication skills to be perceived as a professional law enforcement officer, a challenge that many newer and younger officers face every day. This combination of inexperience also brought with it a perception of cockiness that I had to overcome and learn to recognize.

Over the course of the next two years, I made a reputation for myself as the cop who took everyone to jail and wrote everyone a ticket. Lawrence became known as a speed trap. I was quite fond of this reputation, though, and touted our lack of major crime and our proactive criminal patrols as a deterrence to crime.

As in many small jurisdictions with relatively low crime rates, the primary function of a patrol officer in Lawrence was traffic law enforcement. In this situation, citizens sometimes get the idea that cops have nothing better to do than stop people. They fail to realize the huge amount of deterrence to crime that traffic law enforcement actually accomplishes.

As a result of proactive criminal patrols, our crime prevention efforts resulted in a high number of arrests for misdemeanor and felony warrants, carrying concealed weapons, drug trafficking and possession, drunk driving, transporting/possession of alcohol, stolen auto recoveries, and miscellaneous traffic violations. It also generated a lot of citations written for traffic violations.

As a result of my enforcement efforts, I received the 1991 Mothers Against Drunk Driving (MADD) State of Michigan award for being one of the top drunk-driving arresting officers in the state. The drunks were certainly plentiful in this small Midwest town, since the main businesses on the weekends were two bars overflowing with patrons. The Red Arrow, frequented by the local Mexican migrant population, was especially busy. Across the street, at the Mavericks Tavern, the customers were only local and mostly white patrons. Both bars are now out of business, and the buildings they occupied stand vacant.

The Red Arrow was a haven for drunk and disorderly complaints, bar fights, and stabbings. The owners were frequently assaulted during these fights, but the locals didn't seem to mind the noise; we never received any complaints about the bar from local residents. It was commonplace to have a weekend bar brawl. I never had a problem taking into custody anyone inside the bar during a fight. Perhaps I was just lucky at this point. The fights inside this bar were like something from an old western movie. Literally, the entire bar would be in a bottle-breaking, stool-smashing fight, leaving destroyed property, assault victims, bloody faces, and jailed offenders in its wake. It was so common for a weekend brawl to occur at the Red Arrow that the local mariachi band just kept playing its songs throughout the massive fights.

My proactive criminal patrols seemed to be making a few in the criminal element a little uneasy. In February of 1990, there was a petition circulated by the owner of a video rental business to have me removed from my position as a police officer. The petition read: "We, the undersigned registered and qualified voters, and residents of the Village of Lawrence in the County of Van Buren, and State of Michigan, hereby respectfully, petition for the removal of Officer Todd Christensen for harassment and unprofessional conduct in the line of duty."

I believe it was the search warrant we executed on the business for selling illegal fireworks that put him over the top. A whopping ten people signed the petition. It even made the headlines of the local newspaper, the *Courier Leader*. However, I had more support to keep me employed by the community than to have me fired. A background check of those who signed the petition found them to have either been arrested by me or cited by me for a traffic violation. Perhaps it was their way of finding some sort of redemption for being found in violation of the law. I have the utmost respect for the local village council though. They didn't cave in to the pressure by the criminal element and insisted I stay in the department and continue to enforce the laws I swore to uphold.

The mayor at the time insisted that his officers were to continue to do their jobs and serve the community of Lawrence as police officers. Still, this petition was an eye opener, or should I say instead, a punch in the gut for me. Was I really doing a good job? I began to question myself. What was I was doing that was so terrible it made the very people I swore to protect hate me? I knew I had to start looking for a new place to work—one that would appreciate me as an officer who had the work ethic and desire to reduce crime and improve the quality of life for the citizens I served.

My heart was set on the city of Kalamazoo. Three of my personal friends had been hired by Kalamazoo, and their stories of how they were encouraged and acknowledged for being proactive in criminal patrol motivated me to put all of my energy into getting hired by that city. I knew that, if hired, I'd never have to look for another job. The Kalamazoo Department of Public Safety would be the job of a lifetime for me. But I was only twenty years old, and Kalamazoo would not hire me until I turned twenty-one. I didn't let this fact prevent me from applying, though, because I knew I would turn twenty-one and be eligible by the time the hiring process ended.

Traffic stops for defective headlights, taillights, speeding, and other traffic violations resulted in many handguns being taken off drivers and passengers in Lawrence. It was not uncommon to pull over a motorist for a traffic violation and see a handgun when the driver popped open the glove box. Sometimes the butt of a gun could be seen sticking out from underneath the seat or in the waistband of the driver or passenger. These encounters certainly kept me on edge during all traffic stops.

Guns were commonplace in Lawrence, even before the concealed-weapons laws permitted people to carry them in Michigan. It was not uncommon for me to find a handgun on a bar fight suspect or inside vehicles and on persons during traffic stops. I should point out that these perpetrators were not law-abiding citizens by any means. Most were wanted for warrants or in connection with other crimes, had just been involved in violent criminal acts, were transporting or in possession of narcotics, or were arrested for drunk driving.

"County three-two-two, I need backup at Red Arrow and Butcher Road. Man with a gun. I have him at gunpoint!"

On September 1, 1988, I stopped a vehicle for speeding on the west side of town at Butcher Road just off Red Arrow Highway. The driver, a minister from nearby Bangor, opened his glove box, and I spotted a small handgun. His son, a seventeen-year-old, was in the front passenger seat. My initial response was to draw my weapon and scream obscenities at the driver: "Put your fucking hands on the roof, god dammit. If you go for the gun, I'll blow your fucking head off!" This approach proved most effective on previous similar stops when I spotted a gun in the car, but I soon found out that there's a much more professional way to handle these situations. The driver insisted on showing me that the handgun was not real and several times began to reach for the weapon. My verbal tirade escalated as I yelled at him that he would be shot if he reached for the weapon.

I screamed into my radio for backup and had both the driver and passenger out on the ground lying prone and waiting to be handcuffed when backup arrived. I came to find out, the gun was a fake. It was not an actual pistol but a toy. No arrest was made, the gun was confiscated, and the driver was released. The driver pointed out that he had tried to tell me the gun was not real. I argued that there was no way for me, or any other officer, to know simply by looking at it that it wasn't real. Consequently, considering the threat of deadly force, the last thing we would do is allow a suspect to pick up the weapon. He didn't understand my rationale at all and felt he had done nothing threatening toward me.

The minister, of course, complained about the verbal abuse and emotional trauma he endured during the incident to the chief of police and the village council. The mayor was at first upset, but when the chief showed him the replica handgun, his anguish turned to agreement with my actions. He realized there was no way Officer Todd could have known it was a fake weapon.

To prove this point to the village council, he brought the fake gun to the council meeting without anyone else on the council knowing he had it. With the room full of citizens at a public meeting, including the upset minister, the mayor started the meeting off as usual. Then, before the minister could begin his rant about Officer Todd, the mayor pulled the fake pistol from his pocket and pointed it at the council members and citizens in attendance. He began yelling, "Nobody move, or I'll shoot everybody!"

Well, he certainly got his point across. He went on to explain that this pistol was the gun Officer Todd had seen that night in the glove box. He testified to the citizens in attendance and the council members that there was no way the officer could tell the object was not a real gun. The point hit home. This incident would certainly make national news in America today, but the minister was laughed out of the meeting, and I was found justified in my actions. However, the mayor did have some choice words for me and asked why I had to swear so much during the traffic stop. It was this situation that made me take a second look at my verbal tactics and question my level of professionalism, or should I say, unprofessionalism in a high-risk/crisis situation. As I look back, I realize I had poor academy training to prepare me for these types of situations and simply did what I assumed was right. Clearly, I was wrong.

I would agree that my choice of profane language could have been toned down, eliminated, or modified to get the point across to any potential violator in a more understandable, loud, clear, and assertive manner. A police officer's verbal instructions must be clear and concise, leaving no doubt in the mind of the offender as to what he or she is supposed to do. For example: "Drop the Gun!" "Don't Move!" "Put your hands in the Air!" "Police! Stop!" are short bursts of language that are clearly understood and don't escalate anger. They also give the officer more time to think, break any tunnel vision, and become more aware of his/her surroundings while portraying a professional law-enforcement attitude rather than anger. Remember, our goals are to go home at the end of the day and to treat all of our community members with dignity and respect, regardless of the law violation they may or may not have committed. *Be a professional.*

This incident also gave me time for self-reflection and allowed time for growth and learning as a rookie cop in Lawrence. I started to realize I had a problem dealing with people when the local prosecuting attorney expressed his concern when reviewing one of my many resisting/obstructing police reports. He explained to me that I had more resisting and obstructing police reports than any other officer in the county. "Todd," he said. "I think you might have a problem talking to people, because everyone you arrest seems to be resisting you."

These words stuck with me for the rest of my career and are with me even now in my retirement. Needless to say, shortly after this conversation the department sent me to my first and only course on how to talk to people. I attended a one-day course in Lansing, Michigan, called "Building Your Image through Effective Communication." It helped me realize my faults. Interestingly, the other officers present were all ordered or "volun-told" to attend the training. Like me, they had a large number of assaults against them and complaints by citizens that the officers had treated them poorly and were disrespectful to them.

The course was by no means a silver bullet, but it helped. It took twenty-five years of dealing with people to hone these skills, and they continue to grow even today. A police officer must be a master of communication, a manipulator of words, and an expert in nonverbal communication. It's said that you can talk your way out of most situations, but you can also talk your way right into confrontation just as easily.

Although the early years of my career were relentlessly difficult, I owe a huge thank-you to those significant people in my life who helped me begin my career. Without their personal efforts to help out a new rookie, I would never have had the opportunities that this amazing career would bestow upon me in the years to come.

Thank you, Eric Arrans, Brad Shaw, Amerigo Marcelletti, and George Keeler. You were all great role models for me when I started with my new-found passion for criminal justice.

DEATH IN RURAL AMERICA

"There is nothing more powerful than the heart of a volunteer."
Franklin D. Roosevelt

"Lawrence Quick Response, Van Buren EMS,
respond to 322 West James Street.

Report of an elderly female down on the floor,
unresponsive, cold to the touch.
Possibly dead on arrival."

Y ou never forget your first dead person. I entered the home and was directed into the living room, where I saw my first. The elderly woman must have been in her late eighties, still in her white nightgown, and lying facedown on the floor. She was obviously dead. I don't recall the pungent odor of a dead human body, but I remember her grandmotherly perfume permeated the room. She had that perfume smell that only a grandma would have. Perhaps it was my naïve sense of the smell of death.

The house was freezing cold, and I couldn't help myself; I just had the need to feel her skin. She was hard like a doll. Her skin was pale, cold, and hard to the touch. This feeling was forever engrained into my long-term memory. I still see her body in my mind from time to time. When people ask, "What was the scariest thing you ever saw as a cop?" she is one of the many visions that flash across my mind. She really looked like a ghost to me. After this incident, and sometimes even now, I have a recurring dream that she's floating in the air, long gray hair flowing behind her, with her white nightgown waving in the breeze as she hovers a foot off the ground, still dead but upright, simply floating in a room. I can't get her out of my mind, and she's in a long line of dead people that I can put into a military formation in my dreams. Death never really bothered me, but it does haunt me. I don't think these visions will ever go away.

I served not only as a village police officer, but also as a volunteer on the local fire department and emergency medical services unit, or the Lawrence Quick Response Team. Our local fire and EMS department was state-of-the-art. For a small community, we certainly saw our fair share of death and fire.

On a hot Sunday evening around dusk, a young woman fell victim to domestic violence. Her estranged boyfriend decided to riddle her body with bullets fired from a .22 caliber rifle. I arrived with the quick response team to find this woman lying on her back in a dusty gravel road that wound through the Lawrence trailer park next to the local Laundromat.

Her body had too many holes to patch up. With every breath, blood bubbled up from her mouth and nose as she laid wide-eyed, looking up into the sun, and trying to hold onto her life. One and two and three and four. CPR was attempted, but with each chest compression the bright red blood poured out of every bullet hole. Other medics were trying to patch the holes and treat her multiple sucking chest wounds, but for every hole we patched, a new hole would blow out of her skin as rescue breaths were blown into her body.

Here was the first life that would soon be taken away by death as I held her. I could tell she was dying. Her breathing slowed, her gasps for air slowed and then stopped, and her eyes went from wide and panicked to soft and relaxed. Her final breath was a long exhale, and she never took another.

Nonetheless, we continued life-supporting efforts and worked feverishly to bring her back. We continued to patch every hole and continued with CPR. With each new compression of her chest, more blood flowed from her body, and something strange happened. She was bloating up terribly and began to look like the Stay Puft Marshmallow Man. This medical condition is termed *subcutaneous emphysema*. As we tried to breathe life back into her body, the air was forced into the layer of tissue underneath her skin.

We continued our efforts, and I was assigned to assist the flight paramedics with the West Michigan Air Care medical helicopter to fly from the scene to Bronson Hospital in Kalamazoo. Unfortunately, despite all of our efforts, she died.

Even though the victim died a tragic death, I remember that I had a feeling of real accomplishment from being part of this situation. I quickly learned that I thrived in these chaotic situations. What I felt can only be described as a high or a rush from the moment. For most, this would be a terrifying scene, and it certainly was. Yet what I discovered was that I was able to think, take action, and look ahead in the most hectic of situations. I found that by taking the initiative, I provided a sense of calm to the other rescue workers on the scene. I enjoyed being in command of these situations, and it proved useful throughout my career of working in a toxic, violent, and corrosive environment that others would have nothing to do with. The police, fire, and EMS professionals, however, thrive in such turmoil.

———

Another domestic situation turned deadly in Arlington Township. In rural communities it was common for the EMS team to arrive on the scene before the police. This was not the preferred method of operation for the Lawrence Quick Response Team, or any other EMS service, because it's better for the police to first make sure the scene is safe.

On EMS duty, I was about a mile away from the address when I spotted a female running down the middle of the road and waving her arms wildly in the air. The woman was in a state of panic. As I slowed down next to her, she yelled, "I just shot my husband, but it was an accident!" This was *not* what I wanted to hear. I had the woman wait with the ambulance, and I informed dispatch that the female suspect would be with the vehicle. I was hoping the police responding to the scene would hear this radio traffic since she had just admitted to me that she'd killed her husband.

As I entered the front door of the home, I spotted brain matter, teeth, blood, hair, and bone splattered all over the floor and walls. Especially noticeable was the blood splattered all over the closed window blinds. The body lay on the floor across the living room at the end of the trail of blood and body matter. The victim had the back of his head blown off and his face and brain littered the living room floor. Next to him was the double-barrel shotgun used to blow off his head from behind. The woman was subsequently arrested and found guilty of murdering her husband.

Personal injury accidents along the Interstate 94 corridor in Lawrence Township were plentiful. Two of the most deadly vehicle crash scenes that I witnessed took place in Lawrence Township along I-94.

The first involved three elderly people in a four-door vehicle traveling west on I-94. The elderly male driver had suffered an apparent heart attack. He crossed the median and drove head on into the path of a semitruck hauling a double trailer full of gravel. The car came out on the underside of the semi. The truck subsequently rolled over and smashed into some trees. Its driver had to be extricated from the cab but survived. The three occupants of the passenger car all died. This was the most horrific scene I had ever witnessed in my life. Nothing in Kalamazoo compared to what I saw that day.

The interior of the car was a bloody gut pile. The only way to describe the site was that it looked like someone had taken a meat grinder to a cow and threw it all over the inside of the car. The driver had his forehead impaled on the rearview mirror. He was still belted into the driver's seat, but his left arm was ripped out of his shoulder. The front seat passenger was missing her body from the waist up. The only remnants were from her lower torso. Only buttocks with her legs and feet attached remained. I remember that her cream-colored, high-heeled shoes were almost unscathed but coated in blood and guts. The backseat passenger was simply a gut pile. All that were identifiable were detached body parts.

The day was a warm summer morning and, shortly after the crash, I looked back from the truck to see steam rising out of the destroyed car. I knew it came from the freshly killed people. The smell was that of iron from the large amount of blood and guts that blew up inside the car. It was the most disgusting thing I had ever seen. It was so gross that I remember seeing firefighters vomiting alongside the road at the side of their fire truck. It was very traumatic.

This call ended after the state police accident reconstruction troopers finished their investigation. Then our team was tasked with helping the medical examiners remove the bodies from the mangled car. We simply placed three gut piles into three separate body bags. The backseat passenger was literally scraped off the back seat with gloved hands. There was nothing to pick up. I just scooped up guts in my hands and flung them into the body bag. The smell was putrid.

Another terrible crash involved fourteen Western Michigan University students in a van that rolled over on I-94. None of the students was wearing a seatbelt. All but one was ejected from the van, resulting in thirteen casualties in serious or critical condition. This call was my first mass-casualty incident where triage was needed to save the most people possible. At this call the incident management system was used and resulted in what I would call "controlled chaos." I personally feel the situation was handled well. Three local hospitals were used to manage the patients without overwhelming any one medical system. Ground ambulances and medevac helicopters were used to transport patients from the scene. In the end, ten of the thirteen survived; one died on the scene, and two later died at the hospital.

One patient in particular is forever engrained in my mind. The victim looked like a rolled-up bloody carpet between two other bodies tangled together in the middle of the road. The other two were still breathing, yet critical. The third suffered major head trauma and displayed agonal breathing. I made a decision to direct responding EMS personnel to care for the other twelve patients. By the time all the patients had been transported, the unlucky thirteenth patient had died on the scene. Could he have been saved? I doubt it, but what if he could have? I have to live with the decision I made at the time to save as many people as possible, while one person, who was beyond critical, lay alone in the road, dying by himself. This "playing God" does not bother me. Even as I look back, I don't feel guilty and wonder "what if?" I know the decision I made may have helped to save the lives of the others.

This call once again resulted in increased confidence. I realized the major calls, like the gunshot killing and this mass casualty incident, were the ones I felt most comfortable managing. The only way to describe these situations is "exhilarating." I felt comfortable and in charge during the worst possible conditions. This asset would prove most valuable in my career at Kalamazoo Public Safety, where my mental and physical strength would be challenged beyond my wildest dreams.

I was an Explorer Scout at age fourteen, through my teenage years, and into adulthood. Volunteering as a firefighter, medical first responder, and later as an emergency medical technician (EMT), I've always had a calling for service to my community. It amazes me how many of our citizens have a complete misunderstanding of what it's like to be a volunteer firefighter or medical first responder in rural America. The average citizen simply goes about his or her life, bouncing from one obstacle, challenge, and happy moment to the next, assuming that everything is just perfect in his or her world. So many people think the world somehow revolves around them and are totally oblivious to the bigger world around them.

I found in my sixteen years as a member of the Lawrence Quick Response Team and Lawrence Fire Department that there was a completely different breed of people who walk the earth: the volunteers. They are tethered to a pager and drive a personal vehicle decked out with red lights and flashers. Trained at the same level as their full-time counterparts, I'd say they have a higher level of personal dedication to the communities they serve. These amazing people are willing to sacrifice family time, holidays, a day off, and sleep to burst into action at the moment the tone goes off calling them to duty. My volunteer experiences are among the most treasured moments of my life. I developed a foundation for my future as a career public safety officer (PSO) through my experiences and the relationships I developed in Lawrence. I am forever grateful for the bonds and friendships I made in this community.

Even after being hired by Kalamazoo, I continued my service with the Lawrence Quick Response Team for a total of sixteen years, leaving the department in 2004. While on the team, I achieved the rank of chief of the department and made the emergency medical services a passion. The state of Michigan found it appropriate to award me a Special Tribute Award when I left the team.

State of Michigan
SPECIAL TRIBUTE
To
Robert Todd Christensen

LET IT BE KNOWN, that it is with great respect for his successful career with the Lawrence Quick Response Team that we honor Robert Todd Christensen. He has capably served the community of Lawrence through his leadership and we thank him on behalf of the people he has served so well.

Always willing to lend a hand, even if it meant possible danger to himself, Todd became a member of the Quick Response Team 16 years ago. Having gained considerable experience and training, earning the trust and confidence of other members of the team, Todd served as Chief for 11 years. Sound judgment, loyalty and a penchant for hard work are just some of the qualities that he has brought to this department.

Todd has kept one step ahead of the many changes and advancements in his field and is always willing to share his expertise with others. He is dedicated to educating the community in life-saving techniques, annually offering free CPR and First Aid classes to the public. As Chief, he made it a priority that every member of the team maintained their certifications and that each member was Ice Rescue Certified. He worked diligently to form the Lawrence Township Quick response Team into a Basic Non-Transport Service, the only team of its kind in Van Buren County.

*In his 16 years with the department, Todd certainly contributed a great deal
to the health and well-being of the people of Lawrence
and enhanced the fine reputation of the Quick Response Team.
During his career, he came to know firsthand the great dangers involved with
emergency medical response, the overwhelming fatigue of being on the scene,
and the heartbreak of individuals and families faced with injury and loss.
Through all of these difficult times, Todd has proven himself to be
a professional of the highest caliber.
Clearly, his dedication has served the people of Lawrence in many ways.*

*IN SPECIAL TRIBUTE, therefore, this document is signed and dedicated
to commend Robert Todd Christensen for his outstanding service with the
Lawrence Quick Response Team. May he and his family always know the
safety and well-being
he has tried to secure for others throughout his career.*

*The Honorable Mary Ann Middaugh, State Representative
The Honorable Ron Jelinek, State Senator
The Honorable Fred Upton, United States Congressman*

The Ninety-Second Legislature At Lansing, Tuesday, September 7, 2004

LANDING THAT PERFECT JOB

At the outset of his or her career, today's law enforcement officer is well educated and eager to join the ranks of the warriors who came before. In Michigan, the requirements needed to become a police officer can be found here: www.Michigan.gov/mcoles. A candidate should possess these traits in order to help guarantee success in a competitive job market.

Meeting the minimum requirements as listed by the Michigan Commission on Law Enforcement Standards does not guarantee success. It is up to the individual to make it happen! I remember a quote from one of my army leaders: "If it is meant to be, it is up to me."

The true test to getting hired comes during the extensive background investigation completed by any reputable police department. Departments are looking for employees who are what we call a "total package." You must begin preparing for a life in criminal justice during your teenage years, if you're interested in this career. The formidable years from ages fourteen through twenty-one are crucial to the type of adult you're going to be and the type of police officer you might become. Below is a list of ways a future police officer can better prepare for a successful career and one that embodies the attributes of a true professional.

- Begin honing a solid work ethic. This can be done through employment as a youth. Learn the important skills of responsibility: managing your personal finances, preparing for a day's work the night before (e.g., laying out your clothes), keeping your personal space clean and organized, making your own breakfast, packing your lunch, being on time or early to work, and meeting obligations.

Begin at a young age to master these attributes so that they become part of your natural behavior, and hold yourself accountable.

- Avoid trouble with the law. Any criminal activity will have to be explained to potential employers. Criminal activity may ruin any aspirations you have of becoming a police officer.
- Join an organization or participate in organized activities at school that promote success and responsibility—sports, scouts, volunteer groups, and school groups that make you become part of a team.
- Join the Explorers (a division of the Boy Scouts of America) between the ages of fourteen and twenty-one. Regardless of gender, young adults can join the Explorer Post, which is operated by many local police agencies, and learn the attributes needed for success as a police officer while you're still in your developmental/high school years.
- Seek out and join a reserve officer program, offered by many police agencies for civilians to become actively involved in the criminal justice process.

- Join the military and serve your country. The branch and type of service is not so much at issue. What is paramount is your ability to become part of something larger than yourself and begin a life of service. Military service will not only help you become a better person, but also the knowledge, leadership skills, and life experience gained are invaluable and can never be taught in a classroom. Your military service will also give you a cutting edge during the employment application process, as many police agencies place veteran status near the top of any hiring process. Military service will also help pay for your formal college education or a police academy and give you the financial freedom you earned as a veteran, along with the many other benefits of military service, including health-care coverage.

- Associate yourself with other industry professionals. Seek internships in departments you wish to work for, and go on ride-alongs with officers so you know what it's like inside a patrol car and can get a taste of what your future career might be like.

- Get a formal education in criminal justice. Although obtaining an associate's degree will meet the minimum standards, to boost your chances of being hired you should have a bachelor's or master's degree. Higher education will certainly help you down the road if you have any aspirations of becoming a supervisor during your career.

Most of these things can be done before you set foot in a college class or enter a police academy. Your goal is to set yourself up for success and to develop a solid work ethic and a level of personal integrity and profession-alism that will carry over into your police career. You will also find out if becoming a police officer is really meant for you. You may find out that it's not your destiny. That's OK; this is what growing up is all about. However, if becoming a cop is your dream, make it happen!

This plan for landing that perfect job was exactly what I followed. Before I started to explain how I was hired in Kalamazoo, I thought the list might benefit those aspiring to be a police officer. It worked for me, so why not impart my success to you?

When I was fourteen years old and a sophomore at Paw Paw High School, I joined the Michigan State Police Explorer Post and was men-tored by Trooper Gerry Kerns, who was the Explorer Post advisor. Trooper Kerns specialized in accident reconstruction and was an excellent mentor to help inspire, motivate, and develop me into a responsible Explorer Scout. After my first ride-along with the state police, I was hooked and knew that becoming a cop was exactly what I wanted to do. It was then that I searched out my own path to success. I was also lucky enough to have par-ents who supported me in my career choice.

Throughout high school, I helped to encourage my friends to join the Michigan State Police Explorer Post. Many also went on to become police officers themselves or otherwise involved in public safety. I'm hon-ored to say that my friends, without even knowing it at the time, were a motivation for me to become a police officer. We inspired each other. We were a team.

When I turned seventeen, my criminal justice life took off with energy. I had already been involved with the Lawrence Police Department as a reserve officer and had joined the Lawrence Township Fire Department and Quick Response Team—not as a regular member, but more of a local kid who hung out at the station and washed fire trucks. I was bitten by the public safety bug and wanted to learn all I could about anything related to public service.

In the summer of 1986, I had an important conversation with my mother about attending the police academy at Kalamazoo Valley Community College. During our conversation, she told me that she and Dad could not afford to send me to college. Times were tough for our family. My dad was working in the real estate business, and Mom worked as a medical technologist at Bronson Hospital. With three kids to raise and tough economic times, it would be rough for any parent to finance a college education.

I felt OK with our conversation, though, and really didn't expect any of my college education to be paid for by my parents. I've always been a rather independent person, and I knew exactly what I would do, not only to help out my parents but to pay for college: I would join the army.

Heck, why not? I mean, both of my grandparents and my dad were in the service, so I felt it was only right that I serve my country too. Then the army could pay for school and my mom and dad wouldn't have to worry about it. Well, this was all fine and dandy until I showed up at the house with the army recruiter. I needed to have my parents cosign on my enlistment contract, since I was only seventeen years old.

I remember that Mom was crying as she hesitated, but she signed in the end. Mom is Mom and such a wonderful mother. I knew in my heart that she loved me so much that she was willing to allow her only son to enter the army to help me on my journey in life. What a selfless act. It reminds me of God giving away his only son, Jesus, to all of humankind. At the time, I didn't realize this sacrifice, but eventually I understood that it would be the most selfless act I would ever witness. On September 29, 1986, I raised my right hand and joined the US Army Reserve.

My plan was to attend basic training/advanced individual training and then return home in time to start the police academy in March of 1988. The timing was perfect. I enlisted in the army while I was still in high school. Three days after graduating in 1987, I was off to Fort Bliss, Texas, for training. Following basic training I attended combat medic training at Fort Sam Houston, Texas. You see, back in 1986 when I joined, I was one inch too short to enlist as a military policeman, so I chose another option that I felt would help me as a police officer: a combat medic. It was a great choice, although five years later I would transfer to the infantry. All of this hard work paid off, and after I completed the police academy, I was hired by the Lawrence Police Department on May 27, 1988.

I made one huge mistake, though. I didn't complete my two-year degree until 1999 and didn't finish my bachelor's degree until 2012. Still, with luck, I landed my perfect job with Kalamazoo without a college degree and with only military experience and the experience of a working police officer. It's not easy to juggle working a full-time job and attending school on a part-time basis. This path is completely unrealistic today and impossible by today's MCOLES standards. Formal education is now a requirement for a job as a police officer. Get your bachelor's degree!

I do solemnly swear that I will support the constitution of the United States and the constitution of this state and that I will faithfully discharge the duties of the office of Public Safety Officer according to the best of my ability.

On January 10, 1991, I got the phone call of a lifetime. I was offered a job as a public safety officer in Kalamazoo, and I was to start on February 4, 1991.

Kalamazoo is the largest public safety agency in the country because the police, fire, and EMS services are combined into one department. The agency has, on average, a sworn force of 220 officers who serve approximately 75,000 citizens in a city that encompasses nearly 25 square miles.

This was my dream job come true. Everything I had done in life since I was fourteen years old helped me to become a Kalamazoo public safety officer. It was also ideal because I lived only twenty-five minutes from Kalamazoo and would have great pay, benefits, health care, and union affiliations. I could see a bright future in Kalamazoo and one that would also give me the personal security of knowing that I would not ever have to look for another job. I could stay there until retirement.

My aspirations of working for the city came true but were nearly crushed the following week. On January 17, 1991, I was called up to active duty for Operation Desert Storm and ordered to report to Fort Benning, Georgia, to attend drill sergeant school and rebranch to the infantry. On Wednesday, January 22, 1991, I arrived at Fort Benning with two-year mobilization orders for the Persian Gulf War. Operation Desert Storm was underway.

The year 1991 was a very uncertain time for our military. It was the first major air/land/sea campaign since the Vietnam War. Our battalion was to be a cohort unit that would train, deploy to Iraq, and fight together. I was retrained as an infantryman and completed the drill sergeant academy. Then the new drill sergeants trained our first cycle of basic trainees. Our deployment date was estimated for September of 1991. At that time, the draft would begin. We were to be deployed for six months and then return to train those draftees as to how the war was being fought. Fortunately for our nation, the war ended quickly.

Without even being officially hired by Kalamazoo, the department guaranteed I would have my job when I returned from active duty. They certainly didn't have to fulfill that promise, since I wasn't even sworn in or an employee yet. This consideration was just one of many acts of patriotism that Kalamazoo Public Safety would demonstrate in support of our veterans. The Persian Gulf War ended quickly once the ground invasion began. I was released from active duty after the first training cycle.

On April 22, 1991, I was officially sworn in as a public safety officer in Kalamazoo. Ironically that was the same date as my retirement in 2012. This wasn't planned, but efforts by the City of Kalamazoo to reduce budgetary expenses and reduce the deficit led to early retirements for many employees in 2012. Any employee with twenty-two years in service with the city was eligible for early retirement. The city offered to buy out our last three years of service in an effort to cut costs. Also, the city allowed vets to buy back a portion of their active duty time prior to their hire date. I was eligible to pay into the pension eight months of military buy back. This resulted in an adjustment of my retirement date and put me into the eligible window for an early retirement. I was the last person on the eligibility list.

As I reflect and critically evaluate myself as a police officer, I can honestly say that, had I completed my bachelor of arts degree early in my career, it would have helped me become a better officer in the long run. The personal level of commitment and the educational benefits of being in a college classroom would certainly have given me an improved level of understanding of the world around me. Having a bachelor's or master's degree would have given me the educational edge needed to pursue supervisory positions within my agency. Western Michigan University certainly helped to educate me and broadened my understanding of the criminal justice profession. The instructors and staff are above reproach.

CRIMINAL PATROL

*"People sleep peacefully in their beds at night only because
rough men stand ready to do violence on their behalf."*
George Orwell

"You can make this job as dangerous as you want."
Robert T. Christensen

In 1991, a formalized field training program at Kalamazoo Public Safety was nonexistent compared to today's standards. I rode along for two weeks with Officer "June-Dog" June Tanner in zone seven, the southern section of Kalamazoo. June stood nearly seven feet tall and was the largest black man I'd ever seen. He had a natural ability to communicate with the public in what I would call "straight talk." I could hardly understand a word he was saying with his heavy accent, but his gold front tooth would always bring a smile to my face.

June was a chain smoker and filled the car and my uniform with ashes. He would make it a point to start his shift at a 7-11 store, where he would drink a pop and read the headlines of the local paper. He expressed to me how important it was to keep an eye on the local businesses, and he made it a point to meet with different business owners throughout the night. Our two-week field-training program ended when June told me that I knew my way around the city well enough, had a solid understanding of how the department worked, could write a decent report, and could effectively deal with the public. Plus, he felt I should be on my own. I think he just wanted this new kid out of his car.

My first year in Kalamazoo was the most challenging for me. Many officers who are hired from other departments bring along some good and bad habits, but mostly bad. Unfortunately, I had many. In Lawrence I had literally no supervision, but in Kalamazoo, where the ratio of supervisors to officers was one to three, I was scrutinized and "supervised" constantly. It was a good thing, though, because I was held accountable for my actions. The expectation to perform well was validated through my peers, and I was congratulated and rewarded for proactive policing. Comparatively, in Lawrence I was demonized for being a proactive officer. I felt at home in Kalamazoo. I felt part of an amazing crime-fighting team, and I was motivated to do my best each and every day by my supervisors and coworkers.

What was my hardest challenge as a rookie cop? For me, it was not knowing my way around Kalamazoo. I was constantly looking up streets in a map book and had the most difficult time just finding my way around the city. This dilemma is one of the most common challenges for any new officer working in an area with which he or she is unfamiliar. In my nineteen years as a field training officer, I found that learning the streets was the most daunting task for rookie cops. Once a new kid was able to identify the main roads and knew how they divided the city by block numbers, the job became easier.

Knowing your location at all times must be a priority. Before the age of mobile data terminals and global positioning, officers had to do things the old fashioned way by looking up an address in a cross-reference map book (*The Kalamazoo Red Book*). Today, if the technology goes down, you still have to know where you are and where you're going at all times, while having a constant state of situational awareness. Having a map book is critical.

The skills taught at the basic recruit academy make up the foundation of the street survival tactics for an officer. These skills must be maintained throughout your career, as they are all perishable. Remember the basics such as subject control, firearm tactics, and legal updates. Otherwise, what happens when the computers are down? Yes, report writing, traffic citations, crash reports are all going digital, but even with the advancement of technology, a police officer must still know how to properly write out a police report and handwrite a traffic ticket. Technology is a wonderful thing, but always prepare for and know how to handle the basics of the job when technology fails. Consider large-scale disasters, power outages, infrastructure breakdowns, or terrorist attacks on vital governmental operations. Police work will boil down to the human element of the officer and knowing the basics of the job.

Location! Location! Location! This was stressed to me in an excellent way by a supervisor one night. In 1991, I was responding to an area on the city's north side because several officers were involved in a large fight and were requesting backup. As I struggled to find my way around the neighborhood to help my partners, I used my city street guide and followed the trail of streets highlighted in the book while trying to drive lights and siren at the same time. Needless to say, by the time I arrived on scene, other officers had already arrived, and the situation was under control. Two tactical blunders raised their ugly heads that would live with me for the rest of my career. This life lesson would give me the tactical edge I needed to survive the Kalamazoo streets in the years to come.

My street sergeant that day was always on his A game. I'll refer to him as "Sergeant Stripes" as I describe the positive influences he had on me that set a baseline from which I could grow and learn as a new officer. He had a unique way of getting his point across and one that, at first, I didn't understand. I simply thought he was a rough guy. In reality Sergeant Stripes was one of the best supervisors I ever had the privilege to work for.

As I arrived on scene (still running lights and sirens) in my powder blue and white Chevrolet Caprice ("Smurf-mobile" as we called them) Sergeant Stripes walked toward me with his hands on his gun belt, head cocked to the left, and his face turning red. I could tell he was pissed. I got out of my patrol car, and before I could say anything, Sergeant Stripes asked, "What took you so long?" I had no real response other than to tell him I was following the map book to try to find the intersection. With his hands on the edge of my door, he bent down and peered into my cruiser, and then backed up and looked at me straight in the eyes. "Did the city give you a red book?" he said with that serious look a cop gives a criminal when he's interrogating him and already knows the answer.

I replied, "Yes."

"Then use it! And throw that yellow book away!" He continued to lecture me about how I wasn't going to be able to help anyone if I couldn't find my way around the city. He told me to get my shit squared away.

Sergeant Stripes also spotted the open security window in the car that divides the front and back seats and asked me, "Are you trying to get yourself killed out here?" I wasn't sure what he meant until he quickly followed up his statement by ordering me to close the window in my cruiser so I didn't get my throat cut, get my head blown off, or have my cruiser stolen. He then just walked away.

This was the best ass chewing I could ever have gotten early in my career, and it quickly reminded me that complacency kills in this profession. I was lucky to have a supervisor in the early stages of my career who cared enough to point out my flaws and teach me to be a tactical thinking officer. I appreciated his honesty. I would use this same tactic in the years to come when I became a field training officer. Sometimes, being brutally honest with your partner is the best policy.

The 1990s in Kalamazoo, Michigan, were like a battlefield of crime. The drug trade was at its height. Crack cocaine was the drug of choice for street-level drug dealers. Kalamazoo, positioned half way between Detroit and Chicago along Interstate 94, was rife with crime and turf wars between the drug dealers of these cities. Drive-by shootings, assaults, and robberies took place several times each day and night.

A powerful drug trade fed the supply and demand for crack cocaine on Kalamazoo streets. The entire neighborhood I patrolled looked like it was getting ready for a major parade, with groups of people walking the sidewalks and roaming the streets. The inner-city feel of the area was fueled by a massive supply and demand for crack cocaine. With that came all of the fallout crime and the unraveling of the fabric of the community.

The quality of life in the Northside neighborhood was terrible. Nobody seemed to care about anything except getting the next high or making money from selling drugs. Quality-of-life crimes were everywhere: prostitution; street fights; people walking around drunk or cracked out; folks walking down the streets, sidewalks, and hanging out in parking lots drinking liquor; aggressive panhandlers; reckless driving; street racing; and truancy. It was just a mess. For an aggressive, young police officer, it was a place rife with opportunities to fight crime. Kalamazoo public safety officers were the main line of defense in stopping the drug trade in Kalamazoo. The north side of Kalamazoo was filled with hatred toward police when I started my career, and it only intensified after the 1993 Rodney King incident in Los Angeles.

Sergeant Stripes had a natural ability to read the streets. One night, as we began the shift, he ordered the overhead doors on the station closed and the window blinds drawn shut. He said this action was to help eliminate the risk of bullets being randomly shot into the station. It wasn't even thirty minutes later when a blast of gunshots broke the evening silence just two blocks away from the station.

Sergeant Stripes told us earlier that all he wanted to see that night was a constant stream of red and blue lights up and down the main streets to battle the drug dealers and keep them on their toes. He also instilled in us that we were to continuously back each other up on traffic stops and calls for service. "Nobody stops anyone or a car by themselves. Let's not get shot tonight." He was passionate about officer safety and instilled a sense of brotherhood among his troops. I'm sure this is why he was most upset with me when I was delayed in responding to an officer's call for help.

CRIMINAL PATROL OFFICER SURVIVAL TACTICS

1. Always have situational awareness.
2. Know your location.
3. Know your partners' locations, and back them up often.
4. Update dispatch of any change in your location.
5. Be mindful of radio traffic so you know where to respond to as backup, even when on another call.

6. Never leave the divider window open, and ensure it is locked at the beginning of your shift.
7. Own the streets! These are our neighborhoods, our citizens, not the criminals'. *We*, the *cops*, must keep the peace. Our communities are depending on us.
8. Make officer survival a priority!

I spent my first four years in Kalamazoo assigned to the night shift, patrolling zones four and five. I wanted to be in the heat of battle when I was first hired, and Kalamazoo's north side was full of excitement. From 1991–1995, I worked in one of the most dangerous places in Southwest Michigan. The neighborhood is a predominately black neighborhood, but as a white officer, I found that I was able to establish a good rapport. I enjoyed the challenges associated with being a white officer in a black neighborhood.

Of course, I would on occasion be accused of being a racist cop. I found that, in the course of my twenty-five-year career, this accusation was commonplace when dealing with suspects of another race who were looking for any excuse to place blame on the police for being caught and arrested. I took it with a grain of salt and brushed off their anger toward me. I didn't take it in a personal way, because they were just upset at the blue uniform I wore, not the man behind the badge.

This attitude took some practice, but with time I was able to grow some pretty thick skin. In the end, I can honestly look back and say that I treated everyone I arrested with the dignity and respect they deserved. Race really makes no difference when someone is upset with the police. It's merely a personal attack that's typical human nature for people when they feel they've been wronged for some reason. It's a quick and easy assumption to make, but in most cases it's not valid.

A communication tactic I used is what I called the "mirror effect." I would always start a citizen contact in a polite manner and then adjust my demeanor based on that given back to me by the citizen. If I was treated like a piece of shit, the suspect was treated in a sterner manner—not in a belittling or demeaning manner, but I have zero tolerance for suspects who choose to be complete assholes. Even after fighting with a resistive or assaultive suspect, once they were taken into custody I would treat them as though we were never in a fight and would refer to them in a polite and friendly manner. This was the best tactic I found for calming a highly agitated suspect. It wouldn't work on those highly intoxicated or high on drugs. For the most part, however, even people moderately drunk or high will listen to reason.

I fell into a common trap as a new officer by being quick to argue or try to one-up the uncooperative suspect by simply arguing with them. Well, you can't argue with someone who won't argue back. Arguing serves no purpose other than to piss off the suspects and make them hate you even more. Remember, how you treat somebody has an effect on how he or she is going to treat the next officer. Be a professional. Being rude to a citizen will only result in a complaint against you.

HOW TO CALM DOWN A HUMAN BEING

I would open the back door to the cruiser and ask suspects to step out of the car and tell them to walk toward the jail hallway door. I wouldn't touch them. I found that personal touch simply agitated suspects, and it would make them feel out of control of the situation. Don't use this procedure, though, if you feel the suspect is a threat. Always have control of a suspect if the person is assaultive or potentially uncooperative.

I would open the jail door and, while holding the door open, would say, "Please step inside and stand against the wall." Often people would assume I wanted them to stand facing the wall. I would simply say, "You don't have to stand facing the wall. You can relax." This was the turning point and then, with either their identification or my notepad in hand, I would just ask basic questions such as: "Is this your current address?" "Have you ever been arrested here before?" or "Are you doing OK?" Based on the nonverbal reaction, I could typically tell if suspects were going to listen to reason or just continue to be assholes or even potential threats. Normally, the suspects would not respond to me verbally, so I would initiate the conversation and say, in a calming voice, "Well, what's going to happen in here is that we're going to collect your personal belongings, take your fingerprints and photograph, and then have you use the phone so you can try to get out of here."

This statement had a calming effect on them. It eliminated their apprehensions, especially if this was their first time in a Kalamazoo jail. If a suspect had assaulted or resisted me, I would also use this moment to tell him or her, "Look, I doubt you woke up today and said to yourself, 'I'm going to fight with a cop.' So these things just happen. I'm not mad at you. I know you're probably a decent person, right?"

This statement would also result in not much dialogue from the suspect, but what I would get were some facial expressions, a head nod, or a glare. However, after a few moments to reflect, calm down, and make a phone call, a suspect would be in a state of normalcy and nothing like the irate asshole I'd arrested.

In Kalamazoo we would typically fingerprint our own prisoners. Within about thirty minutes after entering the jail, this process would take place. This was an intimate situation, since I would now be holding onto their fingers, and they were standing right next to me. A soft voice and personal touch gave an excellent window of opportunity for me to stop during the fingerprinting and look them right in the eyes for just a brief moment without even saying anything.

This is when magic would happen, and the suspect would open up and apologize for being an asshole earlier. This same person who just an hour ago was fighting to get away and resist arrest was now telling me that he or she was sorry for being an asshole and would commonly say, "Officer, um, Officer Todd, hey I didn't mean to be an asshole earlier. Hey, I'm sorry, man."

I would almost always reply, "Hey man, no hard feelings. I might need your help out there someday. It's all right. We all make mistakes once in a while."

Officers, this is now a great time for Miranda rights and for you to complete the in-custody interview. You'll find that many people will waive their rights and agree to talk to you at that point because you've shown them that you care about them and you don't come across as a threat like you did earlier.

The next event was a five-minute drive out to the county jail. During this time, I always watched suspects in the rearview mirror to see their faces as they watched regular people going about their business in the world outside the patrol car. I played music in the backseat to help calm the suspects' nerves. At the county jail, when the deputies took control of suspects, I would almost always ask if they had any food that my suspects could have, since they were probably hungry. The deputies were great. They would find sandwiches for my suspects.

Once the handcuffs were removed, it was not uncommon for a hand-shake to be initiated by the arrestee, not by me. If no handshake was offered, I would leave with the last word as the cell door was closed. For example: "John, hey, good luck to you, man, and take care." Use the first name. Don't say "Mr. Smith," but be more personal, and be on a first name basis. Don't be all hemmed up on being called "Officer so-and-so." When an arrestee calls you by your title, tell that person to call you by your first name. Remember, you're trying to break down barriers and establish rapport.

I felt a final, friendly statement would make it sink into the suspect's mind that the police were not the enemy and that they were in control of everything that happened that day. Knowing full well that I would most likely have to deal with this person in the future (or if not me, another offi-cer), I hoped this cordial contact would result in a nonresistive or noncon-frontational situation the next time that same person was arrested. It took me a good seven years to figure this out, but it was well worth it.

Around 1993, Kalamazoo stopped hiring PSOs for about a year. Having the lowest seniority, I was assigned to the jail for nine months. It wasn't something I wanted to do, but I found the work to be most benefi-cial, and it helped me grow as an officer.

My job was to book in, fingerprint, photograph, and feed those incar-cerated while awaiting arraignment. In addition, I maintained their protec-tion and provide for their overall safety and welfare. A local parole agent told me one time that the Kalamazoo City Jail was a place of "real justice," so offenders hated being lodged in our facility. Essentially, this meant that it was a jail where one would sit, eat, sleep, and wait out their time until they were arraigned.

The jail was simple. Each cell was small and steel-barred with a heavy, solid-steel door. There was a small slot for putting in food and water and lighting cigarettes. The cell contained a cement slab floor and a raised cement bench for a cot. Some had a steel bench for a bed with a green vinyl-covered mattress and a wool blanket. Each had a closed-circuit camera, metal sink, and toilet. The cells were painted a dull green, except for the violent-subject cells, known as V-1 and V-2, which were painted pink. There were also the "pink rooms"—holding rooms painted pink because that color was thought to have a calming effect on prisoners with violent tempers. I don't think the pink color helped at all, because the violent prisoners remained just as vicious.

There were no comforts of home in the city jail. Our food consisted of cereal, milk, chips, sandwiches, a pastry, and Hot Pockets. The jail was still a smoking jail, which I used as a tool to keep the masses under control. If prisoners were unruly or loud, I would not light the cigarettes they so desperately needed. The lighter was the most effective behavior control tool in our jail.

During the time I was assigned to the jail, I found myself in more use-of-force situations than I can remember. When a violent suspect was brought into the jail by an officer, the suspect would be taken immediately to a violent cell, either V-1 or V-2. The suspect had his or her personal property removed. If the person refused to answer the suicide questions appropriately, he or she was stripped of clothes and given a suicide gown to wear that slipped over the head and allowed the head, arms, and legs to be exposed. We referred to the gown as a "taco suit." That's what you looked like when you wore the padded gown. Such a suspect was still able to move normally but could not commit suicide with it. Even with these antisuicide efforts, many prisoners still attempted to kill themselves while I worked the jail. One such attempt is forever engrained in my mind.

Officer Don McLennan, who was an excellent officer, was working jail duty on the night shift when I came up to relieve him so he could take his sixty-minute break.

As he made his final round and checked on the prisoners, I heard Don screaming for help. I ran back to one of the cells and saw bright red blood all over the floor. The prisoner had some type of stint in his arm that was supposed to help with blood flow. He had pulled the tubing out of his arm and was bleeding to death. Most of the blood in his body emptied out onto the floor.

This wasn't the most disturbing sight I ever saw in the jail though. Another suspect, who must have been a mental patient, tore his own scrotum with his fingers and pulled out his testicles from the scrotum. Blood was pouring out all over the floor, but the man sat calmly on the bench with his own testicles hanging out of his body.

Another crazed maniac, who was in the violent cell, did his best to try to escape. He took a running start of five feet, ran head first, and rammed his skull into the thick security glass of the cell. He struck the glass so hard he actually splintered the glass with his head. This was his last head strike, though, as he split his head wide open, exposing the top of his brain. He lay unconscious on the floor until an ambulance crew took him away.

In the back of the jail, two cells were set aside and outfitted with more comfortable mattresses and curtains to block out the sun. These cells were set up so officers had a place to sleep. Sometimes a night shift officer had to stay to wait all day long for a court appearance that may or may not take place. I actually enjoyed sleeping in the jail on court days. I could sleep, get paid, and still work that night on patrol without having to take comp time because I didn't get any sleep. I can honestly say that I probably spent more time in jail than a lot of my arrested subjects. To me, though, it was my second home and I loved it.

The jail, my cruiser, and the department were part of me. I found myself at home and in a state of comfort when I was at work. It was truly a home away from home. I felt so attached to the station that I was given a brick from the foundation when the building was demolished in 2003. My dear friend and coworker, Sergeant Julie Yunker, picked up a brick out of the rubble and gave it to me as a gift. This brick meant a lot to me and signified a wonderful piece of KDPS history. I look at it often and enjoy wonderful memories of the old headquarters building.

I would highly recommend that an officer spend a certain amount of time working in a correctional setting. The advantage of such work is that you have the opportunity to deal with the criminal element in a controlled environment and you learn who they are, what they've been arrested for, and how they behave when confined. You learn to respect people in a humane way when their liberties have been taken from them and they're incarcerated. You develop a sense of street smarts by learning how to read people, especially a predatory human being. You gain an understanding of personal respect and dignity that an officer can learn, understand, and appreciate only when in control of another human being who is confined. It will help you become a better street cop.

CRIMINAL PATROL WILL TOUGHEN YOU UP

I worked the city's Northside neighborhood and the central business district during my first ten years in Kalamazoo. From this decade are my most memorable events of violence and death. In this section I'll share with you my personal experiences and feelings about the most memorable calls for service in my career.

"Radio to Baker Forty-one."
"Forty-one, go ahead."
"Report of a taxicab blocking traffic at Church and Ransom."
"Forty-one, Ten-Four."

Nothing sounds unusual about this call, right? Except, it's 1992 in what was then ground zero for prostitution, drug sales, drive-by shootings, assaults, and the related violence that breeds in a crime-ridden neighborhood. This particular call came in shortly after midnight.

I arrived on scene to find a yellow cab stopped in the middle of an intersection. The taxi was riddled with bullet holes, windows were shot out, and the driver was slumped over into the passenger side of the front seat, filled with bullet holes, and covered in blood. He was obviously dead. A robbery? A drug deal gone bad? Rival gang violence? It's hard telling what brought such a violent death to this man, but one thing was for certain. Firearm violence was ravaging Kalamazoo and did not ever seem to let up. Street-level violence had taken over, and it seemed like there would never be an end to the violence.

"Radio all units. We are receiving multiple nine-one-one calls of shots fired in the area of Woodbury and Ada."

I answered this call to find a car that appeared to have crashed head-on into a power pole at Ada Street. The driver was suffering from multiple gunshot wounds to his head and chest. It turns out that this man was a high-level drug dealer and no stranger to Kalamazoo police.

"Radio all units. Engine three and life EMS are responding to a subject suffering from a gunshot wound to the head on Mills Street."

Here, officers found another well-known drug dealer shot to death. This time it wasn't as a result of a drug deal gone bad but rather domestic violence. This victim met his fate with a single gunshot wound to his head fired by his wife. The wound was so fresh when I arrived on scene that the bright red blood was still flowing out of the side of the single bullet hole in his temple region. The bullet made a perfect circle in the side of his head, and the blood was draining out like an open faucet onto the floor. The weapon used, a Glock handgun, lay on the floor next to the three-hundred-pound man. The wife was subsequently arrested in the front yard for the murder.

"Radio all units. Report of a bank robbery, city of Parchment. Suspect vehicle described as an older green Plymouth with a loud exhaust and heavy smoke coming from the muffler, occupied by two male subjects, one white and one black,
last seen Southbound on Riverview."

I was approaching Riverview Drive just as the suspect vehicle crossed in front of me through the intersection, traveling southbound. Several patrol cars converged on the felony stop at the same time. Fortunately, no gunfight took place, but a sawed-off shotgun was seized from inside the suspect vehicle. I remember thinking there were so many cops who arrived so fast that the suspects really had no chance to fire off a single round at the police. Police tactics, however, took a big nose dive during this stop, because patrol cars filed in from all directions, including down range of where any gun battle would have certainly taken place. Officers would have been unable to effectively engage the suspects, simply because other responding officers were not thinking tactically and were rushing into the scene. Fortunately, no shots were fired by either police or suspects during this incident. This incident took place in 1993 when the level of tactical training was still lacking.

"Radio Zone Two, start for Howard's Party Store. Report of an armed robbery in progress. A shotgun was used. Be advised the suspect just shot a victim at the phone booth!"

This robbery would be the last for this suspect. His violent assault against the public and the police would end with him dying by police gunfire and lying in a pool of his own blood in the street on this rainy night. Before he was killed, though, he had robbed a store, shot an innocent victim at a phone booth, carjacked a woman going home and stolen her car, led police on a high-speed chase through the city and county of Kalamazoo, and shot a sheriff's deputy. He changed the lives of everyone involved in just a split second each.

I was training rookie officer Jason Colyer when we responded to the armed robbery call. The scene was rapidly changing, with dispatch continuously updating units from the first responding officers. The suspect had fled the scene after the victim at the phone booth was shot, and the entire shift converged into the area. As we scoured the neighborhood for the suspect vehicle, dispatch received a report of a carjacking less than a mile from

Howard's Party Store. The original suspect vehicle was abandoned, and the robber was in another car somewhere on the city's south side. The officers at the scene of the carjacking reported finding shotgun shells inside the original vehicle. The new suspect vehicle description was updated to units.

It was only a few minutes later when a Kalamazoo County sheriff's deputy reported that he was traveling behind the suspect. The radio was full of traffic as officers, eager to join in, coordinated their efforts to respond. Street Command immediately took control of the chaotic radio traffic and assigned only certain city units to join in the pursuit, thus controlling city resources.

Controlled chaos and managed adrenaline is the best way to describe what happens during these situations. I can only describe what took place inside my patrol car with PSO Colyer. Jason told me he was very familiar with the county road layout in the eastern and northern part of Kalamazoo County. With that, I switched places with my rookie partner and turned the keys over to him. I remember telling Jason, "You drive, and I'll shoot!" I unlatched the shotgun from between the seats and press checked the chamber just to make sure I had a live round. The chase was on. Officers reported the suspect vehicle was increasing in speed and fleeing from police.

The chase continued north around the city limits of Kalamazoo. In the course of the chase, the pursuing units advised the suspect was traveling, at some points, well over a hundred miles per hour, running stop signs, failing to yield, running other cars off the street, and making dangerous maneuvers in an effort to elude the pursuing officers. Dispatch also advised that they received a nine-one-one call from inside the suspect vehicle. The suspect was talking to dispatch and explaining to them that he had taken a hostage at gunpoint and was forcing the hostage to drive the car.

Meanwhile, PSO Colyer and I made our way toward the city's north side as the pursuing units reported they were approaching Douglas Avenue, where the suspect vehicle was traveling southbound back toward the city.

The shift lieutenant broke in on the radio traffic and said, "Lincoln Two to all city units. If the suspect vehicle comes back into the city, R-two is in effect. Take them out. I repeat. R-two is in effect. Take them out!"

This meant that, based on the totality of circumstances, the shift lieutenant had determined that the suspect was a clear and present danger to society. He possessed the ability, opportunity, and jeopardy to meet the requirements of a deadly force assault to end the pursuit and resolve the dangerous situation.

The suspect had already proven his willingness to kill by shooting an innocent bystander during the initial robbery. He had then carjacked a getaway vehicle at gunpoint then led officers on a dangerous chase with no regard for human life. To make this chaotic situation worse, the driver of the suspect vehicle was allegedly a hostage and was being forced to drive.

Moments after the shift lieutenant gave the authorization for deadly force, the situation was over. The result was a deputy shot, the suspect dead, and a second suspect taken into custody. The suspect vehicle had been rammed by police and stopped. The suspect stepped out of the vehicle, leveled his shotgun at sheriff's deputies, and fired his weapon, hitting one deputy. In return, police gunfire erupted and the suspect was shot. The driver was ordered out of the vehicle, arms raised, and taken into custody without incident. The incapacitated suspect was handcuffed, and medical assistance was called to treat his injuries. He was pronounced dead at the scene.

As the mass of patrol cars came to a stop, the gunfire erupted, the smoke settled, with a cop shot and the suspect gunned down. Verbal commands rang out, with guns off safety and fingers at the ready to fire again. "Put your hands up. *Do it now!*" Yelled an officer.

PSO Colyer and I took the driver into custody. The suspect driver/accomplice was transported to the city jail, where PSO Colyer and I conducted the initial Miranda interview.

This scene can only be described as "controlled chaos." What were the cops thinking? What was running through our minds, you might ask? How can anybody want to do the job of a police officer, knowing full well that in the blink of an eye his or her life could be over? Why on earth would someone want to do this for a living? We cops all have our own answers to these questions, but none of these questions came into my mind. It is more than just a job to a police officer; it's our duty to protect others. We don't think about the fear or think, "Oh my God, what if I die?" This possibility does not enter our minds. We are constantly thinking of how to end the madness the best way possible. You cannot allow fear to enter your mind at any point. It's all about winning the confrontation. There is only one rule: *win.* Losing in not an option.

As cops, we thrive in the most corrosive and toxic environments society has to offer. It seems that when we function in a fast-paced, destructive environment, we are at our best. It's during the slow and mundane aspects of the job that we find ourselves making stupid mistakes and allowing complacency to get the best of us.

"Radio fifty-one and fifty-two, start for the area of Kickapoo Court. Report of a subject stabbed with a sword."

Yeah! Sword fights always have two losers. The first loser gets stabbed with a sword, and the winner goes to jail for murder. Two Middle Eastern men decided to take their 1995 New Year's Eve celebration to a whole new level of disagreement, via a sword fight inside an apartment. Put a steel sword through the heart of another person and try to do CPR on that. It's a bloody mess. With each chest compression comes a gusher of bright red blood. There is no stopping that.

New Year's Eve was the strangest holiday to work. Before midnight, the calls for service were almost nonexistent; the night was calm with anticipation of the chaos that would soon follow after the clock strikes midnight. With that, it was common practice for all officers to stay off the streets around the midnight hour. Why? Because every yahoo in the city loves to ring in the New Year by firing guns into the air—or down the street at the police. Once I learned this hard lesson, I never forgot it in my career.

In 1994 I found myself in the city's Eastside neighborhood. As the witching hour approached, I could hear the celebratory gunfire starting to erupt from all around. Most memorable was that, since the Eastside neighborhood is located on a hilltop and with no leaves on the trees in winter, it was easy to look down into the Northside neighborhood. As the gunfire erupted, I saw (and heard) a battlefield image that one would usually see only in a war zone. I heard the familiar sound of machine gun fire and spotted the blast of red tracer rounds, one following another as they spurted from ground level up into the crisp night sky. "Holy Shit! Where the hell did they get that?" was the first thought that entered my mind. Second was, "I'm getting the fuck off the street and into the station."

As I wheeled into the back parking lot of Station Four, I remember seeing the other officers and my sergeant hanging out at the back door. As I stepped out of my cruiser, one of the more seasoned officers said to me: "Hey Junior! Are you fucking crazy? Get the fuck off the street, dumb ass!

Give them about ten minutes to shoot their wad, and we'll go back out there."

"City Baker Seventy-one, respond to 2200 Logan for an elderly woman who believes someone is in her house."

Upon hearing this call, I thought to myself, "Yeah, right. This is just some old lady who has dementia." Besides, at six thirty in the morning who the hell calls police for this crap, right? I could not have been more wrong. This would turn out to be the scariest call of my career—not from danger, but from ghosts!

I thought it was weird as I walked through the front yard and noticed knives hanging from a tree. Certainly not something you would normally see in someone's front yard. So then I was thinking I was dealing with a crazy woman. I knocked on the door. It opened up only a crack. This little old lady was peering at me through the opening.

"Who is it?" she asked in her quiet voice.

"Police, ma'am. Did you call us?"

"Please come in," she replied.

As I entered her home, I noticed it had the usual smell of an elderly woman—that perfumed, body cream smell that a grandmother would have. She was in her nightgown and said not a word, but walked away and motioned for me to follow her. I walked behind with eyes wide open, hand on gun, ready for something to jump out at me. The situation just had an eerie feel about it that I can't explain. I noticed, too, in every closed door there were more knives pushed into the door jams by the doorknobs. I was thinking to myself, "What the hell is going on here? Has she lost it?" I wasn't even thinking about the danger of all of the edged weapons around me, and yes, I was an idiot for not calling for backup right away.

She took me to a spare bedroom door then suddenly stopped and said to me, "He's in there!" She backed up and pushed me toward the door. I stopped her as I saw three steak knives pushed into the doorframe at the handle again.

"Why do you have knives pushed into the doors?" I asked her.

"It's the only thing that keeps him in the room!"

I was thinking, "What the fuck is going on here?" The hair on my neck instantly rose, as if someone had brushed his or her hand ever so lightly against my skin in almost a tickle. I spun around and yelled at her, "Don't touch me like that!" The woman wasn't behind me though. She was sitting on the edge of her bed about ten feet from me. "What the hell just touched my neck?" I said.

She just stared at me—silent, watching.

I pulled out each knife, and then stopped before I opened the door. I asked the woman, "Who's in this room?"

She told me it was a boy.

"A boy?"

"Yes, and he won't leave me alone."

"Well, who is he? Is he your grandson?"

"Oh no, he's the paper delivery boy, but he's dead now."

"What!"

She said it again. "He's dead."

Oh my God! I took a big swallow and my mouth was dry. I started to question myself. It was at this moment that I heard something that haunts me still. A bouncing ball sound was coming from inside the room. My heart was racing, and I was starting to believe this lady. Reality kicked in, and I thought someone was actually in the room. This woman wasn't as crazy as I had thought. I jerked out the knives and opened the door.

It was a perfectly made up spare bedroom. There was a small single bed, a nightstand, and a small chair. There were no windows and only a throw rug on the wood floor. No toys and no bouncing ball. The hardwood floor made perfectly good sense to me because, if a ball was bouncing on the floor, it would make the distinct sound of a plastic ball bouncing on a hardwood floor. The closet was empty except for two metal hangers. Nothing was under the bed. The room was notably cold, however, which I thought odd, since the rest of the house felt like it was nearly eighty degrees.

After searching the room, I pulled the small wooden door closed.

The woman immediately stood up and asked me to put the knives back into the door. "So he doesn't come out," she said. She took the knives out of my hand. Her hands were trembling as she carefully pushed them back into the slots of the doorframe.

At this point I was feeling pretty freaked out, and I believed this lady. I asked her to tell me about this boy who was in her house. She told me that many years ago a small boy was hit and killed by a car in front of her home. He was her paper delivery boy. Over the past several months, his spirit had been in her house, haunting and scaring her by running around and playing with his ball.

I was thinking to myself, "What can I possibly do to help this lady?" Besides that, I felt as though her house really was haunted.

To help calm her mind, I pulled out my pepper spray and pretended that I was spraying the outside of the spare bedroom door. I told her that the spray I was using had an adverse effect on the supernatural, and it would help send the spirit boy up to heaven. I told her she would not have to worry about him anymore. I had used this trick before on emotionally deranged people and was hoping it might work to help calm her mind. However, I didn't stop there. I gave her a victim's rights card that we provide to victims of crime and told her to contact the prosecutor's office. I figured that perhaps they could find a minister to help in the removal of the spirit from her home. As soon as I gave her this card, I got the hell out of that house. Call me a little crazy or whatever, but I believe in that stuff, and I felt if I stayed in this house any longer I could get possessed.

When I left the home and closed the door, the wind picked up, blowing the leaves across her lawn, and all of the dangling knives from the tree were cutting violently back and forth in the wind. I ran to my cruiser and got the hell out of there.

That call didn't end there though. It was about a month later when the Kalamazoo County Prosecutor's Office called me. They wanted to know my thoughts about the situation, because this woman actually called them. I told them what had happened to me. Out of compassion, I believe they followed up on this noncriminal case and referred her to a specialist who dealt with the paranormal. Then, a few more months later, they called to tell me that the woman had a person come to her home and perform a ceremony to remove the spirit, and that was the end of it. This is hard to believe, but it really was a damn haunting.

WE RUN TO THE SOUND OF THE GUNS WHILE OTHERS FLEE.

I was parked at Rose and Ransom (R and R as we called it), my zone partner's cruiser side by side with mine. We were talking about who knows what, when the sound of gunfire pierced the summer night. I can't put into words what multiple gunshots sound like, but the distinctive snap of small arms fire came from downtown. The buildings caused an echo of the gunshots, making it nearly impossible to tell where the gunfire actually came from. We soon knew exactly, however, as the downtown beat PSO, Officer O'Strander called out the gunfire at the Dazzles Night club.

When we heard Dave call out the gunfire at Dazzles, we tore out of the parking lot and raced to the scene. I decided to come up from the back parking lot. I was thinking that if there was a shooting at the club, those involved would try to escape and flee toward the back parking lot. I was right. As I walked through the lot, it was as though I was a shark swimming into a school of small fish—a crowd of hundreds of people was running in my direction as more gunfire rang out near the building. The screaming crowd ran past me, exposing a speeding vehicle and more people running across the street away from the gunfire as the cops were running toward the sound of the guns.

In the middle of all the commotion was PSO Ron Jennings. He was in the street in a shooting stance with his handgun pointed at a speeding vehicle coming right at him. The driver slammed on the brakes, and officers converged on the vehicle. The passenger tried to flee on foot, but he was tackled and slammed against the side of the car. As he was being handcuffed and searched, a handgun was found tucked in the small of his back. One suspect in custody.

FOOT PURSUIT TACTICS

"Fifty-one city foot pursuit, eastbound through the backyards from the apartments. Black male, blue jeans, white shirt, red hat!"
(Unit number, in foot pursuit, location, direction of travel, suspect description.)

I activated the emergency lights of the patrol car, but the suspect vehicle fails to pull over. Instead, it increased in speed and turned into the driveway of an apartment complex. The siren of the patrol car is wailing, lights flashing, and suspect vehicle is fleeing. All the while I'm trying to radio dispatch my location, the fact that I'm in a vehicle pursuit, vehicle description, license plate, reason for the traffic stop, speed, and direction of travel. The suspect vehicle drives behind the apartment complex and is trapped by a fence and there is no way for the car to escape. The driver now jumps out of his car and is on the run. He is sprinting toward the back of the lot and struggles to climb the fence.

Meanwhile, I've slammed on the brakes and jammed the cruiser's gear shift into park while the car is still in motion. The cruiser struggles to come to a stop as a loud clicking sound is heard from the transmission and the seatbelt locks me into the drivers seat while the car slows down. I'm trying frantically to unbuckle the seatbelt so I can jump out of my patrol car to give chase to the suspect.

Finally, out of the cruiser and I'm in a sprint trying to catch up to the fleeing suspect. Up and over the fence, running through the backyards. I yell out: "Stop Police!" The suspect runs around a house and is out of my site. I can't see the suspect running through the dark, but I can still hear him climbing over a chain link fence as he runs across the top of backyard rubbish and metal. The dogs in the nearby yards are barking as the commotion of the foot chase alerts them to our presence and I catch a glimpse of the suspect as he jumps another backyard fence; Unfortunately, I have no idea where I am. I'm simply determined to catch him, fight with him, and arrest him. I'm also not calling out my location to dispatch *as I should* be and backup units have no way to find me as they struggle to set up any type of perimeter to help contain the suspect.

The sirens are ringing out in the night sky and I can hear the heavy acceleration of nearby patrol cars. Still, I don't know where I am and once again I've lost sight of the suspect. Anticipating an attack by the suspect I draw my weapon. I'm quickly shining my flashlight through the dark trying to spot him again. I stop running and just listen to my surroundings. I am hoping to hear him running through the yards, or making a noise, listening for anything to clue me in as to where he might be.

With my handgun at the ready I turn off my flashlight. In my mind I'm considering the fact that the suspect has stopped running and is waiting for me. Why? An ambush! His option now is to lay in wait and attack me, or wait for me to pass by so he can escape undetected.

There he is! Hiding on a small porch by the back of a house and he is crouched down underneath a small table. I yell out to him: "Let me see your hands! Come out now! Slowly!" I radio dispatch: "Fifty-one city I have the suspect at gunpoint. I'm behind a house, but I don't know my location, I think I'm near Staples Street."

While I'm talking on the radio the suspect leaps out from his hiding spot and runs directly at me. Just before he tackles me I strike him in the side of the head with the radio and he falls to the ground, then struggling to get to his feet. I holster my weapon and jump on his back to try and gain control. The fight is on and he's rolling toward me, not to escape, but to assault me. He manages to get the web of my left hand in his mouth and is biting down hard. Wham! I strike him as hard as possible on the side of the head a second time with my portable radio. The radio sparks and breaks in half. This was devastating to the suspect and took the fight right out of him. He was then handcuffed and I walked him out from the backyard to the street.

Still, nobody knew my location and I had no backup. I could hear my street supervisor, Sergeant Dave Headings on the public address system from his patrol car: "Todd, where are you? Let us know where you're at."

In the end this was a successful apprehension. But, there were several foot pursuit tactics that I learned from this incident and employed these tactics in my future foot pursuits that helped ensure success.

- Know your location at all times.
- Update dispatch and responding units when your location changes.
- When in foot pursuit speak loud and clear into the radio and *don't scream*.
- Announce you are in foot pursuit, location, direction of travel, and suspect description.
- Carry a tactical flashlight on your gunbelt when working day or night shifts.
- Anticipate a ground fight and end it quickly when you catch the suspect.
- Have control of the suspect in less than thirty-seconds.
- Have control before you handcuff.
- Carry two pair of handcuffs.
- Have the will to fight and win every confrontation.
- Maintain proficiency in ground fighting tactics.
- Always watch *deadly hands*.
- Consider wearing tactical gloves during criminal patrol.
- Wear lightweight footgear than is conducive to running.
- Maintain a high level of cardiovascular and strength endurance.

During my career in Kalamazoo, I was involved in a number of foot pursuits. So many I can't remember all of them. One thing to keep in mind is that many of these foot pursuits can be avoided by becoming an expert in reading non-verbal communication and have control of every suspect during police contact. One tactic that I found that worked time and time again was to simply have good control of everyone you are taking into custody. Assume that when you take hold of someone they will attempt to resist or assault you. Just tell yourself this: "When I grab onto this guy he will turn around and break my nose on the first punch."

Be assertive, speak confidently, commanding, and have control of everyone you touch. Any moment of weakness in your level of control will be interpreted as a *leak* in your ability to effectively control a suspect and if detected by someone who is willing to escape, looking for an opportunity to escape, or anticipating a moment to elude you they will do it!

"Radio Baker Fifty-two, respond to Burrell and Lawrence. Report of a group of juveniles throwing rocks at an abandoned house and breaking out the windows."

Doesn't sound like much, right? Well, take a screaming juvenile into custody on a hot summer night in a crowd of people who hate the police and are just looking for a reason to attack you. That's exactly what happened to me. This simple call turned into a deadly force situation and caused the responding officers to abandon the area as we took a barrage of rocks and bottles from a hostile crowd that grew from only a handful to nearly a hundred pissed-off people.

When I arrived near the scene, I spotted one of the juveniles standing in front of the abandoned house throwing rocks at the front picture window. As I walked toward him, he was oblivious to the fact that he was being approached by a police officer, and he continued to hurl rocks at the window. There were a few random people wandering the streets; situation normal. However, when I grabbed the kid by the arm and started to handcuff him, all hell broke out.

The kid started to scream, which caused the few people wandering in the streets to take notice and begin to yell at me also. "Just let him go. He didn't do anything!"

I ignored the yelling and escorted my juvenile offender toward my car and placed him in the back seat. As soon as I turned around, I had a very irate female screaming in my face and insisting I let this boy go. Somehow they were related. The scene was turning ugly.

I yelled at this woman, "Back off or you're going to jail too!"

She said, "Fuck you, mother fucker! I'll whoop your mother fucking ass, you white pig bitch!"

Well, here goes the neighborhood. I tried to arrest her, but she took off running. I grabbed her by the arm, but her momentum carried both of us along as I tried to get the cuffs on her.

"Fifty-two radio, ten-nineteen!" (Send backup!)

I yelled for backup as she was clearly going to be a fighter and the ever-growing crowd got larger and louder. I caught up to her as she hit the sidewalk just a few yards away at a fence. With one hand, she had hold on the fence. My attention was drawn to her hand holding onto the fence while the crowd was starting to encircle me, and their yelling intensified. I could hear glass bottles hitting the street around me.

"Fifty-two radio, I'm taking bottles. Step it up!"

This was no small woman. I'm talking a solid, two-hundred-plus-pound pissed-off female, and she had no intention of letting me take her to jail. She had a death grip on the fence and, unknown to me, with her other hand she had a hold on the grip of my pistol. As I glanced down and saw she had hold of my gun, a Sig Sauer P226 nine millimeter, I also saw that the snap of my holster was undone, and she was actively trying to pull the gun from my holster. With my right hand I put all the weight I could onto the gun to keep it in the holster and was screaming at her, "Let go of my gun, or I'll blow your fucking head off!"

She was screaming at the top of her lungs to the crowd, "Help! Help!"

"Let go of my fucking gun, you goddamn bitch, or I'll kill you!"

I kept my backup weapon, a Walther PPK 380 semiautomatic, in a vest holster located on my left side. I had replaced the buttons on my shirt and installed a zipper just in case I needed to get to my backup gun quickly. This was that time. Actually, it was the time I should have shit my pants, because here I was in a deadly force confrontation with this crazed woman trying to disarm me. I was holding on for dear life to keep my primary weapon in the holster and, with my left hand, trying to unzip my shirt to get to my backup gun and shoot this bitch in the head. However, I could not reach inside my shirt to unholster my backup gun, because it was on my left side and my right hand was required to keep my other gun in the holster. Had the gun been on my right side, it would have been easy to reach in with my left hand and shoot her in the head.

PSO Bob Zuniga came running up from behind the suspect and was pulling on the arm holding onto the fence.

"She's got my gun in her hand. Get her off me!" I yelled.

Bob pulled her down to the ground by reaching around her neck and pulling her head backward. Success! Now the neighborhood was in total chaos. Rocks, bottles, sticks, anything that could be thrown was coming in from all directions. Sirens were wailing in the background, and more units arrived. All the while, Bob and I were handcuffing this woman on the ground.

Just then, Sergeant Tom Martin, commander of the Tactical Response Unit at that time, came up to me and said, "Todd, you get her in a car and get the hell out of here, *now!*"

The police were completely outnumbered, and there was no calming this situation. It had gone too far and the neighborhood was in an uproar. The female was taken to a nearby cruiser and transported to KDPS headquarters. All of us left the area with bottles and rocks impacting around the ground and onto cruisers as we left the scene. What a fucking mess!

It wasn't over yet. When we arrived at HQ, my female prisoner was complaining of chest pain and trouble breathing and was claiming to be having a heart attack.

"Oh my God!" I thought.

The shift lieutenant, Don Verhage, didn't waste any time. "Get an ambulance here now. Take her to the hospital, and we'll deal with it there."

In the end, she had had a panic attack and did her best to avoid jail.

I don't know what the charges ended up being, but she promptly filed an excessive force complaint against me and the other officers involved. Her claim was that she was beaten with nightsticks, and her face was rubbed in dog feces while she was on the ground being handcuffed. None of this was true. I think the inspector appreciated my honesty during the internal affairs investigation, though.

As I was explaining to him what had happened, I expressed my concern that I was unable to shoot her while she was trying to disarm me of my primary weapon. I also told him that perhaps I could have used less profanity when I was telling her to let go of my gun. The investigation revealed that I did nothing wrong, and I was exonerated from the excessive force allegations. I didn't even carry an impact weapon (nightstick) back then. We had been issued a wooden hickory club for an impact weapon, but it never left my car. Tactical mistakes? Absolutely.

Although I was faced with two distinct deadly force situations during my career where I would have been justified in using deadly force, as I look back, instead of Monday morning quarterbacking myself, I can honestly say that I was lucky enough to survive both of them without having to actually use deadly force.

Two vicious dogs, however, were not as lucky as my human suspects described previously. On a warm summer evening, a frantic elderly female pounded on the door of the Bryant Street station. Covered in blood from a gaping wound in her leg, she said, "I was in my garden and was attacked by a dog!" A brown, shepherd-type dog had attacked her. We all recognized the woman, as she lived directly behind the station. Station PSOs went into action and bandaged her wounds as an ambulance was dispatched. Meanwhile, Sergeant Merlo and I went out to find the vicious dog.

I armed myself with the Remington 870 shotgun from my patrol car and changed out my ammunition from slugs to buckshot. As we made our way down the alley, we spotted the animal. It trotted out from behind a garage and took off into a backyard area where its attention was drawn to other dogs. Animal control officers had been called to our location in an attempt to capture the dog.

As we stood in the front yard area with the vicious dog in the backyard, pacing back and forth with other dogs, barking, and panting, Sergeant Merlo told me, "Todd, if that dog comes at us, you shoot that thing!"

It was only minutes later when Kalamazoo County Animal Control officers arrived. I informed them that the dog had already attacked a woman, putting her in the hospital, and that the animal was behind the house. Armed only with a snare, the daring animal control officer walked into the backyard.

"Todd, go with him!" commanded Sergeant Merlo as he stood near the other side of the house, handgun at the ready. A crowd had gathered across the street as they watched with curiosity.

I followed slightly behind the animal control officer as he walked toward the backyard with confidence. The vicious dog was barking in a rage as the officer made his approach, snare held out. The dog took off running at the control officer who tried to lasso the running animal, but missed. Then the dog was running directly at me. I fired the shotgun and knocked the dog down with the first shot. He stood back up. The second buckshot round ripped his guts out, and he fell dead in the curb of the road. When the dog fell, several members of the crowd began to clap and cheer.

In an ironic twist, some of the pellets of the first buckshot round that hit the dog had also penetrated the nearby foundation of the house. This turned out to be the home of the vicious dog's owner. During the incident the owners were not home, but during the officer-involved shooting investigation by the Office of Professional Standards (Internal Affairs), the owner came home and was informed that his dog had attacked his neighbor, who was currently in Bronson Hospital. The owner admitted that his dog was aggressive. He was cited for harboring a vicious animal and allowing his dog to run loose.

A second vicious dog met his maker in a similar way when I responded to a burglar alarm at a business. The call came in at the beginning of the shift in the dead of winter and with a blizzard raging outside. The last thing I wanted to do was deal with this alarm, which I assumed would be a false alarm. That turned out to be a terrible assumption on my part.

As I made my way around the building in the blinding snow, checking doors and windows for any signs of entry, my assumption of a routine call quickly turned into a deadly force situation as a white chow mix security dog came charging at me through the snow and leaped at my chest in attack mode. With no time to run, my only option was to draw and fire. With a gloved hand, I drew and fired a round into the dog's head and one into his chest as he leaped into the air at me. I tried to move backward as fast as possible in the knee high snow. The dog dropped at my feet and died instantly.

I had a backup officer on scene who had been checking the opposite side of the building. When he came around the building, he asked: "Hey, did you hear a gunshot?"

"Yeah, I just shot their guard dog!" I said. The dog was tethered to a rope on a pulley system that allowed it to patrol the entire area near the entrance.

Once again, another officer-involved, shooting investigation took place, and the inspector came to the scene to hear my version of what happened. After I explained to him why I shot the dog, he chuckled and replied, "Well, at least this time you didn't cheat with a shotgun like last time."

As an officer, I felt pretty good about both situations—not that I'd killed two dogs, but that I didn't miss with my shots! As officers, we train, train, and train for deadly force situations. When you're successful in any use-of-force situation (deadly force, less lethal, or while handling assaultive/ resistive subjects), that increases your level of self-confidence about your ability to perform immediately under pressure and in a life-threatening or potentially life-threatening situation. Plus, I was happy to know that I would not be teased by my partners for firing my weapon and missing. God knows, if you shoot and miss, you'll never hear the end of it from your fellow officers.

Officers must carry every piece of force equipment available to them. The modern day officer should be equipped with all use-of-force equipment items: weapons, backup weapons, knife, impact weapon, chemical spray, Taser, and tactical flashlight. Carry all the tools of the trade! Be creative in your carry positions and practice accessing your weapon systems in different scenarios.

We make this job as dangerous as we want. I hope that every cop who reads this will come to realize this reality. *We* really do make our job either safer or more dangerous for ourselves.

Why do we continue to put ourselves into harm's way without even thinking of the consequences of our actions? The following is a list of poor behaviors:

- not wearing seatbelts
- driving recklessly
- not observing our surroundings
- not thinking "big picture"
- rushing into scenes

- running on scene
- parking our patrol cars in front of the call instead of walking in on foot
- not wearing our bullet resistant vest
- not having a backup gun on our person
- eating poorly and not staying in good physical shape
- failing to attend continuing training
- not practicing effective defensive tactic techniques
- not being familiar with ground fight training
- not going to the range often and not just to qualify, but to actually become experts in our shooting ability
- turning our backs on people
- approaching a traffic stop on the driver's side when on a busy highway
- not calling for backup when you know you should
- becoming complacent
- not stopping for a stop sign or red light when running code and then killing an innocent person or even our own
- driving so fast that you lose control of your patrol car and kill yourself or your partner
- jumping into a water rescue without wearing a life jacket
- failing to do a thorough search of a suspect
- wearing low-level security holsters
- standing or walking between your patrol car and a suspect vehicle on a stop
- failing to call out your traffic stop or citizen contact
- not knowing your location

Why do we do these things listed above? We've all done them. Tell me *why*? You all know the answer. Tell me and tell yourself why, and stop doing them. It all boils down to the basics we all learned in the police academy. Don't lose your tactical edge with longevity; maintain it and build upon it throughout your career. Sure, we will all make mistakes. Learn from them, learn from each other and be as tactically sound as you can.

Insist that your partners do the same and inspire them to do great things. Appreciate each other, praise each other, and take care of each other. Don't let mistakes continue to be repeated. You don't need to be any type of command officer to make this happen. A seasoned officer has just as much influence on the troops as any command officer and, in many cases, even more. Be a leader!

Dispatch: Public Safety Emergency. Do you have an emergency?
Caller: Yes, I've been stabbed.
Dispatch: How did you get stabbed?
Caller: A black guy broke into my house and stabbed me.
Dispatch: Really? Do you know this guy? Where is he?
Caller: No. Well, maybe. I think he is a friend of mine.
Dispatch: Where is he?
Caller: He's gone.
Dispatch: Where are you stabbed?
Caller: In my side.
Dispatch: Sir, police are on the way along with an ambulance.
Caller: OK.
Dispatch: So, tell me how this happened to you. Tell me how he got into your house. Did he break in or was he visiting?

This was an actual nine-one-one call that I answered while working relief in our dispatch center. Do you see anything wrong with this conversation? To the untrained eye, perhaps not. However, the experienced criminal justice professional should recognize a problem. You guessed it. The person who called nine-one-one made up all this. Further, there is a sad twist to this incident.

As the call was being taken, our department responded as though this was an actual emergency. Officers arrived on scene to find the alleged victim suffering from a stab wound to his abdominal area. Yes, he was really stabbed. However, the investigation couldn't locate a suspect. Police tracking dogs were sent to the scene. Several officers searched the neighborhood and set up on perimeter points, all in an effort to catch the attacker. I'm sorry, but, "A black guy stabbed me." Come on, now! We can see right through that one. Nobody calls nine-one-one like that. Unfortunately, this is our society and yes, the caller was in fact a white guy blaming his alleged assault on a black guy. When I heard this claim, I knew something was just not right with the call. There were no signs of a break in at the home, and his descriptions of the suspect and the situation had not stayed true to his original call to police.

After I completed my hour-long tour of relief dispatcher, I went back to my patrol duties and drove straight to the hospital. I had a hunch this guy had made up this story for some reason when he called nine-one-one, and I wanted to know the truth. Why the hell would he make this up? I had no idea at the time, but I did know that if he was lying to me, he would be charged with filing a false police report. In this case that meant a felony.

I arrived at the hospital and found two other officers in the trauma room with our alleged victim, who was suffering from a stab wound to his abdomen. I asked the other two officers to leave the room for a moment while I spoke to the victim.

I stood next to the hospital bed and looked into his eyes. He was alert and seemed to be in no pain as he lay on the hospital bed with his bleeding controlled. The hospital staff was in no rush as his wound wasn't life threatening.

"How you doing?" I asked him as I observed his injury.

"I'm OK," he replied.

"I'm the officer who answered the phone when you called nine-one-one tonight."

"Yeah?" he said.

I looked at him right in the face and I told him, "I don't want you to talk right now. I just want you to listen to me while I tell you something." He closed his eyes and just lay there.

"John, I don't know what really happened to you tonight, but I'll tell you something. You know, I've been a cop for several years, and I've seen a lot of people stabbed, shot, beat up, and fucked up, whatever. But I have to tell you, I can pretty much tell when someone is not being completely honest with me. Now, I don't know what's running through your mind. But I do know one thing. What you told me about being stabbed—that never really happened did it?" As I was lecturing him, he squeezed his eyes tighter, and I could see tears starting to flow from the corners of both eyes. He moved his head, and I could see that my words were about ready to hit a home run. The truth was about to come to me. I kept talking. "Sometimes, we just get caught up in life and maybe it seems like there is nothing else we can do or say, and we just can't go on or we get confused and frustrated." I reached down and put my hand on his shoulder.

In a situation like that, use personal touch, keep talking, close the personal space, don't be loud, talk compassionately with a voice of understanding, watch his nonverbals, don't let him talk yet, and keep explaining how you understand because the confession is about to come.

"John, look at me! I'm not going to arrest you. Something happened tonight to you. Tell me."

Give him a way out. He feels compelled to tell the truth. He needs to vent.

He turned his head toward me with tears streaming down his face. "I didn't know what else to do." As he cried, he swallowed, and through his crying, words came out.

"I...I just need help man. I need help. I got this." He paused and looked down to his side. "I got this fucking bag on my side; I shit in a fucking bag!" His voice raised and I looked down toward his side. "I shit in a bag! And I need help, but..."

"But what?" I asked.

"I can't afford my medication anymore. It just hurts so bad, and I need another surgery to fix my guts, and I can't afford it. My fucking doctor won't approve me. So I thought..." He paused. "I thought if I..."

He took a deep breath and it was like a breath of relief. "I thought if I made up the story of getting stabbed, they would have to do surgery on me, and they could fix me so I wouldn't hurt anymore. I just want to go on, man. I just want my surgery and some meds. I need some help."

"So, John, I have to ask. Nobody really stabbed you tonight did they?"

"No. I'm sorry. I made it all up. But I had to. I didn't know what else to do. I'm not in trouble am I?"

"I told you I wasn't going to arrest you, right? I meant that. I'm not. You're gonna be all right. Now, I don't know what the deal is with your doctor or why you can't get that surgery, but let's just see if we can get you patched up tonight, OK? And maybe this will help you get the help you need. I appreciate you being honest with me."

I feel that this call was important to share, because it says something about cops that people fail to realize and that we, as cops, sometimes overlook or forget about: *compassion*. The great thing about police work, though, is that so many police officers practice acts of compassion each and every day, and we do it out of a genuine feeling of love for humankind. To protect and serve with compassion is what it's all about.

Did I charge John with the felony false police report? You bet I did, and I explained his entire situation in my report. The prosecuting attorney's office had this same level of compassion, even though a charge had been brought against the victim (now suspect) in this matter. That's what I loved about the prosecuting attorney's office in Kalamazoo County. They don't just randomly charge and prosecute, but they seek out justice. Isn't that what it's all about? Justice! I hope John got the help he needed to live his life, and I hope he learned a valuable lesson.

I mentioned that this investigation took place because I had been working as a relief dispatcher as part of my regular tour of duty as a street officer. A critical link in the criminal justice profession is that of a public safety dispatcher. As a citizen, you call nine-one-one and you expect immediate and courteous service, right? Well, of course you do. That's exactly what our dispatchers are charged to deal with. However, what you don't realize is what happens on the other end of the phone line. I'll do my best to honor the dispatchers I was so fortunate to work with for so many years, but as an officer there is no way that I can be completely accurate in my description of these unsung heroes. You call nine-one-one, and someone says, "Public safety emergency. What is your emergency?"

Emergency! Let's repeat this: nine-one-one is not an information line as you'll find out immediately when the emergency dispatcher rattles off the nonemergency number and hangs up on you. Why, you ask? Because you're not the only person calling nine-one-one, and there are only a limited number of emergency lines available. That's why you might actually get a busy signal at times, because every nine-one-one line is being used. It's not a limitless supply of telephone lines like one might think. To make matters even worse, many of the nine-one-one lines are not even being used for actual emergencies. So what is an emergency? Before you, as a citizen, dial up nine-one-one, ask yourself these questions: Is this a life-threatening emergency? Do I need police, fire, or medical intervention right now?

If the answer is yes, by all means call for help. If not, you could be putting someone else's life in jeopardy by taking up a nine-one-one phone line when there is no emergency. So, you've called in an emergency. While you're on the phone with the dispatcher, police, fire, or EMS is automatically notified and sent to your given situation. Meanwhile, the dispatcher is continuing to ask you vital questions so that responding emergency personnel are updated as to the changing nature of the emergency. Call after call after call, our dispatchers are prioritizing and triaging each emergency and nonemergency call that comes into any given dispatch center. In addition they're handling the communication between the dispatch center and responding units to coordinate an efficient and proper response to each emergency as presented. A dispatcher is truly a unique individual and is a master at communication, listening, and multitasking. He or she can truly make the difference between life and death. A commanding dispatcher who controls chaotic radio traffic is paramount, and I'm proud to say that the dispatchers of Kalamazoo Public Safety are by far America's best.

Let's prepare for criminal patrol. I'll give you the secrets of my daily preparation for patrol so that you can learn how to formulate your own effective habits to better prepare yourself mentally and physically for criminal patrol.

It starts out with a good night (or day) of sleep—ideally eight hours of sleep, but let's be realistic, that's not always going to happen. Nonetheless, you have to take care of yourself before you can take care of someone else. Now wake up! Your shift starts in four hours and it's already three in the afternoon. Wake yourself up with a solid workout before your shift even starts. Go for a run, bike, swim, do strength training or a cardiovascular workout. Get moving! Think to yourself, "I'm going into battle, and I have to be prepared to win."

You've gotten in your daily workout. Now, have a healthy meal before your shift starts and make your future lunch or dinner before you walk out the door. Avoid restaurant food while on patrol. Make your food and bring it with you. It's cheaper and, in many cases, much better for you. Besides, you can keep it with you in your cruiser throughout the shift. Drink water and have water in the car. The last thing you want is to get hungry or thirsty. Keep the metabolism pumping and stay hydrated.

I would always arrive thirty to forty-five minutes before my shift started. You still have a lot of preparation to do before you get into your cruiser and go into harm's way. I would go to my locker at the station and change into my uniform. This is where you mentally prepare as you put yourself into "cop mode." You are transforming from citizen to police officer, and in your mind you are thinking tactically. As you put on your uniform, bulletproof vest, and gun belt, you inspect each item so that it is in the proper place. I would always conduct a press check of my handgun to ensure I had a live round in the chamber. I wanted to know with my own eyes that I had a round in the pipe. Agitate your pepper spray, battery test the Taser, inspect your impact weapon, double check magazines, function check patrol rifle and shotgun, verify radar/laser, and inspect the patrol car and all patrol equipment. All the while you are mentally preparing your mind and your gear.

Before each shift began, I would also say a prayer as I signed onto my mobile video recorder, and it went just like this: "This is Officer Christensen, employee number 1319, on duty as Baker Sixty-one from 1900 to 0700 hours. Dear Lord, please keep our officers safe today. God Bless America and the US Army."

Now, I was ready to go and early! One reason to be early was so that my opposite shift partner could be freed up if needed and so that he or she could get out of work on time. The remaining time would be spent checking e-mail, getting a fresh cup of coffee, and visiting with my coworkers. Then followed the shift briefing and off to patrol.

TRAFFIC LAW ENFORCEMENT

Most "good people"—those citizens just going about their daily lives and routines—usually come into contact with a police officer only when they wave at them during a parade, see them on television, or find themselves being pulled over for something that, in their mind, they didn't do. Typically, these traffic stops are a result of a traffic violation, or perhaps an equipment violation that they had no idea existed on their vehicle, such as a taillight, headlight, or license plate light burned out.

The traffic laws in every state are miles long—seemingly never ending. In fact, I would wager that most cops don't even know all of the violations that exist on the books, since they differ from state to state. So how would any motorist possibly be educated in all of them? Regardless, traffic law enforcement takes up a large chunk of time in a police officer's career. The goal here is to simply create a safer driving environment so that people don't die. That's the easiest way to put it—so people don't die.

Still, from the citizens' point of view, cops are out to get them in regard to speeding and the like. You know what? They're right. Our job is to find those breaking the law and stop them. The end goal is to prevent poor driving habits and unsafe acts that lead to traffic crashes. Speeding and intersection violations seem to be the most common contributing factor to traffic accidents.

Beyond that, guess what? There are a multitude of arrests that come from stopping cars. What do we find among the motoring public from a police officer's point of view? Illegal drugs, drug traffickers, people wanted for anything you can imagine, drunk and drugged drivers, illegal weapons and guns, those who just committed a crime who are leaving the scene, and drivers who have been forbidden to drive (suspended, revoked, denied). The list goes on and on. If you think about it, how else does the criminal element move around? Besides walking, or riding a bike, they are in motor vehicles. How do illegal drugs and guns get into and across the United States to your neighborhood streets? Yes, in a motor vehicle. So, as the law-abiding citizen reading this book, open up your mind and think about the big picture of what a police officer is hunting for. It's not just to write you a speeding ticket. We are digging, searching, and looking deeper into the traffic stop than you can ever imagine.

Most people are not intentionally speeding. They simply lose track of time and space and have no idea how fast they're really going. This is why, in Michigan, traffic violations are civil infractions and not a criminal violation. The laws also require only that the officer prove by the preponderance of evidence (51 percent) that the violation occurred and not beyond a reasonable doubt as in a criminal case. Another assumption so many speeding violators make is that the speed they were clocked at is the speed they were going when they hit the brakes after spotting the police. The reality of it is that the police see you speeding and have measured your speed well before the speeding driver ever notices the police officer.

A traffic stop for a civil infraction violation (speeding, disobeying a traffic signal, defective equipment, etc.) may be the first time this citizen has ever come in contact with a police officer. We must make this initial contact a professional experience. One that leaves in the mind of the citizen is the thought, "Wow, that officer was very polite," regardless of whether or not a citation is issued. If you, the officer, are not already starting out your initial contact as in the example below then give it a try:

"Good afternoon. May I see your driver's license, please?"
"The reason why I stopped you was _____."
"Do you have your vehicle registration and insurance?"

Remember the mirror effect I talked about earlier? Always start out polite and professional; adjust your demeanor as needed, depending on the situation, since every traffic stop is different, just as all people are different. Here is a common mistake so many cops make. Not only is it unprofessional, but it implies that you, the officer don't know why you're pulling someone over. Also, it leads citizens to believe that you are trying to trick them into admitting that they have done something wrong. Again, don't start out this way:

"Hi, do you know why I pulled you over?"
"May I see your driver's license?"

When you start out this way (and I know you do because I've been pulled over myself), you're implying to the citizen that you are an idiot pulling me over for no reason. Even if you have a perfectly good reason to stop me, a greeting like the above implies that you don't. Can you see the difference? Give it a shot. You will find that you are arguing much, much, less with motorists about why they were stopped, and you will have better control of the situation.

From a tactical aspect, having the person's driver's license or ID in your possession should be your first priority. Think to yourself, "If I get shot, then what?" Imagine this scene: You pull a vehicle over, walk up to the driver, explain why you stopped him or her, and then you're arguing with the driver as to the allegations you have made. You don't have a driver's license in your hand and *boom*! You get shot in the face! The driver takes off leaving you dead or bleeding out in the street.

How can you help track down your killer? Get that driver's license in your hand as one of the first things you do when making driver contact and stick it in your pocket. Of course, this can't always happen. Still, it was running through my mind all the time. "If I get shot, then what?" I want my partners to find the suspect's driver's license on me so that the suspect can be caught and held accountable for murdering me. This was just my tactic. If you have a better one, then awesome!

TRAFFIC STOP SURVIVAL TACTICS

For police officers, stopping traffic violators is one the most common job functions we perform. And as I found out, in the beginning of my career, they can certainly be one of the most dangerous situations you can ever find yourself in. Consider the tactics I've outlined below to help better prepare you so that you don't fall victim to the deadly fate so many of our brothers and sisters in our profession have been killed performing.

- Call out your traffic stop to dispatch before you turn on the overheads: location, vehicle plate/description, and number of occupants if more than two. For example:

Unit: "City Baker Eleven. Traffic Stop"
Dispatch: "Eleven, go ahead."
Unit: "Michigan and Rose"
"Charles, Charles, Adam, Two Six Nine Eight"
Dispatch: 23:01 (time)

Tactically, this communication is good, because you're telling dispatch all of the traffic stop information *before* you turn on the emergency lights. That way, if/when the vehicle flees, you have already called out this information and can then focus on the occupants. Remember, update dispatch if your location changes because your next radio traffic may very well be, "Eleven city. Shots fired!" Prepare yourself for this possibility on every stop. Think to yourself, "If I get shot, then what?"

FURTHER ADVICE ABOUT PROTECTING YOUR-SELF WHEN MAKING A TRAFFIC STOP INCLUDES:

- Position your patrol car so that you can effectively use it for cover and adjust this position based on traffic flow situations, especially on busy streets and highways. Reposition your car so that it absorbs a rear-end collision impact to help you survive while sitting in your car.
- Once the vehicle is pulled over, change the overhead lights in your patrol car to rear warning only so that you are not blinded by your own lights when you look back at your cruiser, or if the driver needs to submit to field sobriety tests.
- At night, turn on the spotlights quickly so that you can observe furtive movements inside the suspect vehicle.

- A tactic I loved and learned from the Michigan State Police was to turn on my spotlight during daytime stops and point it behind me toward oncoming traffic to help with warning approaching vehicles.

- Crank those tires right or left depending on how your car is positioned. These are great bullet stoppers and can help provide you with more cover from ground level bullets. Keep in mind that bullets will hug the ground if they are fired under your car. It would suck to get your feet shot out from underneath you. Cranking your tires will also help propel your car away from the traffic stop, if hit from behind, rather than ramming into you or the vehicle you just pulled over.

- Don't slam your door. This is not a game of hide and go seek. So don't slam your door, which is my biggest pet peeve of all time. Simply allow the door to close quietly or leave it still slightly open. You don't want to let suspects know when you're on your way up to their car. On the other hand, though, you might want to slam your door twice on purpose if you are on solo patrol. In Kalamazoo, we were solo both day and night. So, I would slam my door twice and do a passenger-side approach if I had multiple occupants in a suspect vehicle and wanted them to think that there was more than one officer pulling them over. I loved watching them trying to find the second officer who never existed.

- If you are on a busy road or highway, do a passenger-side approach so you can look inside the suspect vehicle without getting hit by a passing vehicle. How many cops getting hit on the highways does it take for us to stop doing driver's side approaches?

- A passenger-side approach is also a great tactic if you are on solo patrol on a stop that you feel is not good. This is when you need to listen to your sixth sense! Here are some dead giveaways that tell you to use a passenger-side approach:

    A. The vehicle is slow to pull over.
    B. You see the driver or passengers reaching down under the seats or other furtive movements that may indicate they are armed.
    C. You see the driver or passengers moving around and really trying to find you in the mirrors.

- On approach, *watch those hands*, and observe, observe, observe! Don't get locked in with looking at the eyes of the occupants. Your goal is to observe the interior of the vehicle for weapons and contraband to further your investigation and keep from getting shot.

- Ask yourself during every approach and while you're standing at the door this question: "How can I keep from getting shot when they start shooting?" Once you're in position, stay slightly behind the occupants so that they have to turn their heads to see you. Keep the "B post" as your friend. This post is the vertical doorframe between the front and back doors; it may be your only piece of cover. Always watch the hands. At some point, when you feel it is safe, you need to make a step forward to view under the driver's seat from the front to give

89

you a better view of the center console and under the front of the seats. It takes only a quick moment to take two steps forward while viewing this area and inspecting the VIN plate and the dashboard.

- Driver: "I don't have a driver's license, officer." Arrest the driver now! You have an arrest, so make it. You need to positively identify this person before you decide to cite and release or lodge. I'm sure you would hate to let a wanted person go, right? Let's not debate the issue with the driver.

Before I make this arrest, though, I like to make the driver think that he or she might have a way out, so I hand the driver my notepad and pen and have the driver write down his or her name, birth date, address, and social security number. Most of the time, yes, you guessed it, they will lie about the name and write down only parts of the real name. However, on some rare occasions the driver simply left his or her license at home. Either way, that person is coming out of that car in handcuffs and going into the cruiser for a citation or a ride to jail. The great thing about your notepad is that you then have a piece of evidence when you charge the driver with giving you a false name in an attempt to obstruct you and disguise his or her true identity.

Remember, that question, "How can I keep from getting shot when they start shooting?" This problem is exactly why you want to make this arrest. If you decide to take down the driver's name and return to your patrol car to try to identify the person, you have to make a return trip back to the suspect vehicle. All that time the driver has been sitting up their thinking, "How am I going to get out of this?" knowing full well you're going to be arresting the driver. This just gives that person an opportunity to plan out an escape or assault against you. Or the driver will just take off, and then the chase is on! Make the arrest, and you can avoid all of these problems in the first place.

- Don't turn around and walk back to your car. You're going to get shot in the back! You needed to learn how to check for traffic and walk backward feeling for the corner of your car and watching the suspect vehicle. If you practice this method, you'll have it down pat after just a few times, and it will become second nature to you. The suspect is watching you walk back to your cruiser. When you don't turn your back, if the driver has dealt with the police before, he or she is going to see this difference and know that he or she will not be able to do anything against you because you are ready for it. Remember, this may be a potential predator you are dealing with, and you must not become the prey.

- If you have not slammed your door but left it open, you can sit down and not close your door all the way. Something strange might happen now. The driver could get out of the car. Now what? You get out of your car, too. Don't let the driver walk back to you and kill you sitting in your car. Meet the driver halfway, or tell him or her to please have a seat back in the vehicle. So what will you do if you sit back down in your patrol car and the driver starts shooting? Escape out the front passenger side door of your cruiser and use your car as cover while you return fire? Throw your cruiser into reverse while staying low inside the car to avoid being shot through the windshield? Put your car in drive and run over the assailant with your car? Maneuver your cruiser away from the shooter and return fire? Shoot through your windshield? These are the scenarios you must always be running through your mind. Options? It's deadly force at this point, so your only option is to win!

- Once you have returned to the suspect vehicle and you're issuing the citation, keep it out of your gun hand.

- If you're solo, call for backup to make an arrest. Why risk it? Time is on your side (usually). Make it an unfair fight. Two against one is much better odds that one on one.

To avoid a fight at the door, consider this tactic: You have an arrest to make of the driver. Instead of having him or her step out of the vehicle, simply tell the person that he or she is under arrest and have the driver spin around in the seat, put hands behind the back, handcuff them, and then have the driver step out of the car. I avoided so many assaults this way. It's an unexpected action that throws the driver off guard. Remember, the driver knows he or she is going to jail, so if you present that person with the opportunity to escape or to assault you, the driver is going to take it. Why risk it? Just say, "OK, sir, there is a warrant for your arrest. You are under arrest at this time, so just spin around in your seat and put your hands behind your back."

- Backup officers, when you hear your partners call out a traffic stop, go to them, or at least start their way. When this is not possible, always have your radio ear tuned in so that when they do call out a stop you already know where they are when they start screaming for help.

It's common to arrive at another officer's stop and just drive by, give a thumb's up, and away you go into the night. Rather, pull up behind your partner, lights off so you don't backlight them, and turn on your rear overheads to add warning to approaching traffic. Get out and be a rock star backup officer. Your mere presence may be the deciding factor if your partner is going home alive that day or not. Don't be complacent. Take the time to do backup.

Officers, don't be so proud that you don't call for backup. Call for backup, please! Whenever I called for another unit on one of my thousands of traffic stops, not once did any of my partners ridicule me for calling. We are a team and here for each other. You want the odds in your favor, so call for backup.

I attended a risk management seminar in 2006 presented by Gordon Graham, of Graham Research Consultants and he offered one of the best quotes I've ever heard that will sum up the issues of officer safety is, "Predictable—preventable."

If, in the course of your career, you simply keep this quote in mind, I know it will help you increase your personal level of officer safety in your daily patrols. For example, if you are responding emergency status in answer to a call and you're pushing that cruiser well over the speed limit, lose control and crash without wearing your seatbelt. It's pretty damn predictable that you'll be killed, right?

In addition to not wearing your seatbelt, another common practice for officers is to affect a traffic stop and approach the driver from the driver's side of the suspect vehicle on a busy street or highway. We can say it's predictable, based on the history of officers struck by passing vehicles, that you're more likely to be hit and killed by a passing car if you're standing in the street at the drivers door than if you make a passenger-side approach and stand out of the way of traffic, right?

Let's take it to another level of common complacency that officers seem to continue that ends in a fatality. If you go on patrol and don't wear a bulletproof vest and are engaged in a gun fight, odds are that if you're hit by a suspect's bullet, you're not going to survive, right? So let's prevent those tactical mistakes that we can predict.

OFFICER DISCRETION AND HOW IT EVOLVED OVER TIME

My personal level of "officer discretion" changed and evolved over my twenty-five years of stopping traffic violators. When I first started out in this career, I felt that a warning was in order for most violators and that it would help with police/citizen relations. In particular, I thought that giving a warning to an upset motorist would somehow smooth things over and that he or she would leave the traffic stop with a more positive outlook upon the police. Boy, was I surprised to find out how fast this behavior would backfire on me. I gave my first verbal warning to a drunk driver in Lawrence. Before you all start to panic, no I didn't just let her drive away. I actually gave this person a ride home and wrote her a ticket for failing to signal. I parked and locked her car on the roadside. Do you see anything wrong with this picture? The year was 1988, and I had been a cop for only one month. I was naïve and didn't realize the possible ramifications for making this dumb decision.

About four hours later, I was dispatched to a crash only a mile down the road from where the original traffic stop took place. You guessed it. That same person I gave a break to came back to get her car and promptly crashed it into a tree as she failed to navigate a curve. You could say that I got a good talking to the next day by the chief after I explained the situation to him. Lesson learned! Arrest the drunk driver every time! Thank

God nobody else was hurt or killed, and, thankfully, the driver herself wasn't injured. This situation would have all been avoided had I simply done the right thing first and made the arrest.

Amazingly, I didn't learn my lesson after this incident. Almost an identical traffic stop took place on the exact same stretch of roadway, and this time I wrote the driver a ticket for careless driving. I had the front seat passenger drive the car instead of the intoxicated female. Back in 1988 the legal limit in Michigan was a .10 percent blood alcohol content, and we relied heavily on the results of the preliminary breath test. The PBT indicted a .10 percent, so I decided to give another break. Instead of arresting the woman for drunk driving, I chose to cite her for careless driving. What was I thinking? Why on earth did I make this stupid decision?

The feeling among other cops back in 1988 was that if you had drunks who blew just a .10 percent, then they really weren't that drunk. It's similar to catching a twelve-inch bass. You know, "barely a keeper." I felt that if I arrested this person who didn't seem that drunk, I could be facing peer pressure from other officers or would be perceived to have an overly aggressive attitude toward citizens and lawbreakers. I know, crazy, right? I should never have let my personal thoughts and opinions influence my decisions when it came to enforcing the law.

I got lucky. No crash this time, and I thought I actually did the right thing. No arrest, the person was off the street, and I still cited the driver for driving poorly. Everything was fine until I received a subpoena to appear at an informal hearing where this same violator was contesting the ticket for careless driving. At the informal hearing, the magistrate heard the case, and I testified to the facts of the violation, including my decision to give her a break for drunk driving. During the informal hearing I mentioned that the PBT indicated .10 percent breath alcohol content. The violator insisted that she wasn't drunk, that I was lying, and that she was driving just fine. The magistrate found her not responsible, and she left with a smirk on her face with words I'll never forget: "You small town cops ain't shit."

The magistrate told me to stay in his office. He took off his reading glasses, held around his neck by a chain, and said, "Well, I hope you don't ever do that again." He had some great words of wisdom for me. "Todd, if you ever have someone who's at or near the legal limit for drunk driving, just arrest them." At that moment I made a career decision to never, never, ever give another break to a drunk driver. It set me on the right path, and I never gave another break to a drunk driver again. I learned that people don't appreciate a break even if you think you are giving them one, and my job is not to drive around and give warnings but to enforce the laws I swore to uphold.

THE DECISION TO ISSUE A TRAFFIC TICKET OR A VERBAL WARNING

So how did I decide to write a traffic ticket or just give a verbal warning? This is a simple answer for me, but every officer has a different opinion on this. I would always issue a traffic ticket unless:

A. You are on your way to the hospital and it is a true emergency.
B. I stopped the wrong car. (Yeah, this happens.) I would always err in favor of the citizen and not risk citing the wrong person.
C. I honestly thought that *you*, the violator, had a really good reason or excuse for breaking traffic laws. Nearly 99 percent of the time, anyone I stopped was cited. I felt that I wasn't getting paid to drive around and stop people to give them a warning. My job was, in my mind to enforce the laws.

1) You are a fellow police officer or a family member of a police officer. Pulling over a fellow officer is very rare by the way, and to those citizens who think professional courtesy means cops are driving around ignoring the traffic laws, speeding, etc., you could not be more incorrect. Police officers are probably the safest drivers out on the road, as we essentially drive for a living and see the results of poor driving habits. Keep in mind, too, that as an officer, in Kalamazoo anyway, if you crashed a cruiser and were at fault, you would be issued a traffic ticket in addition to disciplinary action. Now you know. We are not above the law.

2) The exception to all of the above resulting in a citation no matter who you were: If you were completely disrespectful toward me and belligerent, you would be cited. This behavior would always result in a traffic ticket or an arrest, if I had probable cause to arrest you for any reason. I felt that, if you had what I called a "poor driving attitude," then you probably didn't give a shit about anyone else on the roads, and you were therefore a hazard to the motoring public.

DRIVING UNDER THE INFLUENCE OF ALCOHOL OR DRUGS

"A drunk driver is a mobile homicide waiting to happen."
Robert T. Christensen

On February 18, 1995, I responded to a man down, bleeding, and severely injured. I arrived to find thirty-three-year-old Kirk Hudson lying in a pool of blood and barely breathing, with a severe head injury. Next to him lay his twisted and mangled bicycle, vehicle parts scattered all over the street near his body. Kirk Hudson died on that day, but the investigation as to who killed him was just beginning.

As a result of a detailed forensic investigation and unrelenting investigative police work, the driver of the van that struck and killed Kirk Hudson was found. Evidence located at the scene of the crash would lead investigators to the owner of the van who, fled after he struck Mr. Hudson. The key to solving this crime was a small piece of plastic, turn signal covering that matched exactly to the suspect vehicle. In addition to the exact match of the broken plastic piece were paint chips and other vehicle parts found at the scene and collected as evidence.

The driver of the van was subsequently arrested, prosecuted, found guilty of fleeing the scene of a fatal hit and run crash, and served prison time for the crime. Although his level of intoxication at the time of the incident could never be proven, it was certainly suspected to be over the legal limit. This particular investigation was found to be so unique that it was described in a television episode called "The Plastic Puzzle" on the TV documentary series *Forensic Files* in 2005.

It was said that in Kalamazoo, a homicide investigation was easier to complete than a drunk-driving arrest. This was, of course, not true, but there were some sharp comparisons. The average length of time for a DUI investigation from time of stop to report completion was an average of two to three hours, depending on the presence of any other contributing factors that may extend that time. The shortest amount of time to complete a thorough and well-documented investigation was no less than two hours.

What was it that would make the DUI case a living hell for an officer? Just add any of the following and the time could be extended to up to three or more hours: Breath test refusal, search warrant, traffic crash, blood draw procedures, secondary charges (e.g., drug possession/trafficking, resisting arrest, assaulting police officers, fleeing/eluding, warrants), and generally uncooperative subjects in particular like those who would refuse to be fingerprinted. Overall, dealing with the intoxicated/potentially uncooperative subject is challenging for anybody, including the police.

In the course of my twenty-five years of arresting drunk drivers, I found that I was among the top officers in Kalamazoo who consistently made the most drunk-driving arrests on an annual basis. I pride myself on the fact that the majority of these cases resulted in a conviction of some type. What I learned most about this experience was the importance of attention to detail throughout the investigation, report writing, and courtroom testimony. Toward the later years of my career, I learned from local city attorneys that they actually enjoyed prosecuting my cases and were less likely to plead them down to a lesser offense, because I had developed a reputation of documenting a thorough investigation and being exact in my courtroom testimony.

I wasn't the type of officer who craved a conviction. If I thought the investigation was incomplete in any way, or if I had made a mistake (which was typically the failure to document properly), I would not hesitate to err on the side of justice and lobby for a dropped charge or simply testify to the facts of the case, even if that meant a not guilty verdict. Courtroom integrity was my priority. There were even some cases in which I would admit that an investigation was flawed or that I could empathize with the defendant on why a driving mistake may have been made due to confusing traffic laws. I would never try to hide or cover up anything.

The worst thing an officer could do was to jeopardize his or her personal integrity in the courtroom. This has third and fourth order effects that will destroy your career both on and off duty. Just be honest. If you screw up, learn from it, and don't make the mistake again. I established a solid reputation in court for being an honest officer and one who would tell it like it was. It was a great feeling while on the witness stand when a judge would make remarks in reference to my personal integrity. It was devastating to the defense counsel.

I recall my first drunk-driving arrest in Kalamazoo. Although this was typically what we would term a routine event for any officer, Kalamazoo seemed to add an additional system of checks and balances to how we conducted a drunk-driving investigation. My first arrest took nearly six hours to complete the Kalamazoo Public Safety way.

Since I had worked previously as a police officer in Lawrence, I felt relatively confident in my ability to process a drunk driver in the right way. However, in Kalamazoo, Sergeant John Uribe taught me the finer art of investigations and how a thorough drunk- or drugged-driving investigation should be completed. It was Sergeant Uribe's passion for excellence and his dedication to duty and his troops that established a foundation for me throughout my Kalamazoo career. It was this extra effort taken by a supervisor that helped me grow into an effective public safety officer and instilled a sense of personal motivation to complete every investigation in the most thorough and accurate manner. Attention to detail is key.

Two such cases come to mind. First, back in 1991, I arrested a gentleman for drunk driving and, during the courtroom testimony, the defense attorney asked me to tell the court what the results of the Breathalyzer test were. I replied simply, "Twelve percent." A motion was immediately filed to suppress my testimony because I didn't state that the results showed 12 percent blood alcohol content by weight. Well, we lost the case. Afterward

I asked the defense attorney what I could have done differently to avoid making such a mistake in the future.

He replied, "You have to pay attention to detail and follow the administrative rules. I bet you won't do that again though, will you?" I never forgot this lesson and made it a career goal to never lose another case because of my own mistakes or what is termed, a technicality.

The second case was in my final year in Kalamazoo. The case was dismissed by the judge from a motion by the defense attorney alleging that the reason for the stop was invalid because the defendant didn't break any traffic laws. The incident revolved around the placement of a no-left-turn sign. The defendant had turned left from a store parking lot, adjacent to the intersection. Two no-left-turn signs were clearly posted at the intersection and across the street. I stopped the motorist for the violation. The issue raised by the defense attorney was that the no-left-turn sign wasn't erected properly according to the traffic code prohibiting vehicles from making a left turn from the parking lot, thus making the reason for the stop invalid.

I testified that this was true. There wasn't a sign in the parking lot indicating no left turn, as required by the law. I also testified that, based on the law, the stop was invalid. Now, on the night in question I had no idea what the municipal code was for the placement of traffic signs, and I doubt most officers did, unless they were previously an employee of the public works department and knew what regulations governed sign placement. I had no problem losing this case. The fact of the matter was that it was an invalid stop. Did a drunk driver get away? No. He was arrested on the night in question and, potentially, lives were saved, including his own. In addition, the city traffic engineer learned his lesson in court and would pay closer attention to proper sign placement to avoid losing these cases in the future and to properly direct the motoring public.

In Kalamazoo the call volume was heaviest between four in the afternoon and three in the morning. During this time, if the calls for service were excessive, the last thing an officer would want to do was "bone his zone partner" by arresting a drunk driver. This would mean the other officers would have to take most of the calls for service and/or other PSOs would infiltrate a zone and have to take your calls while you were tied up in the jail with a drunk. We prided ourselves on taking care of our own zones. It was part of our community policing efforts, in my mind anyway, to take care of my own neighborhood. Hell, I knew it better than any other officer coming to take a call from another part of the city.

The downside to this situation was that there were times when drunk drivers would either not be stopped or may simply have been let go by officers who didn't want to deal with the two-hour-plus process of a drunk-driving investigation. Was this the right thing to do? You can argue both ways, but the answer is no. Letting criminals go is not the right thing to do *ever*, especially a potential "mobile homicide suspect." However, there were times when an officer needed to quit stopping cars and concentrate on taking the calls for service in his or her zone. It was difficult, especially in the warm spring and summer, to keep up with just the calls for service. After two in the morning, though, drunks were fair game, and it was expected that they would be arrested and taken off the streets.

When I started in 1991, I remember having over twenty PSOs working the street during the shift. Over the years, through contract negotiations, budget cuts, retirements, and a hiring freeze, this number continued to decline. When I retired in 2012, the minimum staffing level for PSOs was just thirteen officers working the street. You can easily see how staffing levels affect the quality of service delivery for any department. If you don't have the officers to keep up with the call volume, something has to suffer. There were some nights when it was so busy that the shift lieutenant would simply clear the board, so to speak, and we would just start over with a new shift and new calls for service because we could not keep up with the calls that were still remaining. The calls that would simply disappear were nonviolent, quality-of-life calls, such as parking complaints, noise, fireworks, barking dogs, loud music, junked or abandoned autos, and traffic complaints. In other words, we ignored the type of call that, for the most part, was a nuisance call that would result in an officer checking the area several hours later to find nothing going on. We hated to do this, but like a hospital emergency room, we prioritized/triaged the most violent or criminal calls where there was a victim or that required an immediate police response. As the years progressed, the department became much more efficient in responding to each and every call for service in a timely manner and streamlined the reporting system to meet the needs of the public. Of course we continued to search for ways to cut costs and provide quality police/fire/EMS services.

There was a handful of officers who took this mind-set of being proactive in arresting drunk and drugged drivers to heart and effectively saved lives by making many drunk-driving arrests. The officers who truly made a difference and saved lives on the streets were Chuck Dahlinger, Tim Randall, Marty Buffenbarger, John Uribe, Fidel Mireles, and me. Interestingly, prior to being hired by Kalamazoo Public Safety, each of us had worked at other departments. It was commonplace for each of us to make at least one to three drunk-driving arrests in just one shift.

As a result of my proactive patrols and high number of alcohol-related arrests, I was awarded the Mothers Against Drunk Driving Award in 1990 and Police Officer of the Year in 2007 from the Western Michigan University Students Against Drunk Driving organization. Nominations for the Police Officer of the Year award were based on enforcement and prevention initiatives dealing with drunk driving, minors in possession of alcohol, illegal liquor establishment violations (liquor violations committed by local liquor stores and bars), and drugged driving arrests. I pride myself on taking action where many other officers would not. I think that the reason was that many officers just didn't feel capable conducting the investigation in a timely and thorough manner.

To help our troops in this area, I developed a report-writing guide, along with the city attorney, to help educate our officers on how to conduct these investigations and how to document a thorough and detailed police report. I did this through the use of effective headings to give the officers a street guide for attention to detail.

The following is a basic template to use when completing a drunk-driving and drugged-driving police report. Of course, you may need to add headings depending upon your local jurisdiction's standard operating procedures and local prosecuting attorney's guidance.

Summary: No more than three to five sentences.

Traffic Law Violations: Your reasonable suspicions and your reason for the stop.

Contact with Driver: Your initial observations and statements (tell why he or she was stopped).

Driver Statements before Arrest: What the driver said. (At the time of the stop, ask everything you need to know so that, if the driver refuses to answer questions after Miranda, you already have these statements.)

Dexterity Test: Results of the Standardized Field Sobriety Tests (preferred).

Signs and Symptoms of Alcohol Intoxication: What you saw, heard, and smelled.

Signs and Symptoms of Drug Influence: What you saw, heard, and smelled (become familiar with all drug effects on the human body).

Preliminary Breath Test: Results of test (should be given if you suspect drugs; results will show a low or no BAC level).

Arrest: Any out of the ordinary circumstances (resistance, voluntary statements).

Vehicle Search: Reason for search.

Evidence: List of all evidence seized (follow your department SOPs).

Vehicle Disposition: Towed or parked.

Chemical Test Rights: What the driver said when asked to take the breath test.

Breath Test: Any out-of-the-ordinary circumstances and the results.

Search Warrant: Name of the judge (provide the suspect with a copy of the affidavit).

Blood Draw: Search warrant or consent (follow department SOPs).

Miranda Rights: State of driver's mind/ability to understand rights (At arrest, read them off the Miranda card, not from memory), and time read (follow department SOP).

Driver Statements after Arrest: What the driver said (voluntary).

Miranda Interview: Miranda waived.

Witness Statement: Names of all passengers in the vehicle and their statements about the driver's level of intoxication or drug use.

Citations Issued: Citation numbers, if issued (follow dept. SOPs).

Digital Video Recorder: DVR/MVR number.

Before you sit down with your cup of coffee to begin your report, it's paramount that you take the time to review the entire stop from start to finish from your in-car mobile video. You want to ensure you are documenting exactly what you saw from your video and listen to the statements made by the suspects and the questions you asked on video. Take notes! Don't document your report based on memory. Take the time to document accurately. Pay close attention to details, so that you don't contradict yourself in the report. Remember that the video is what the jury and attorneys will see when matching up your police report to the documentation seen on the television. Pay attention to detail. You can lose a case simply because you failed to document accurately what really took place.

RACIAL PROFILING VS CRIMINAL PROFILING

A traffic stop is based on the driver committing a violation of the law, right? Or is it based on race? Racial profiling is a hot button topic for every agency. Does profiling exist? Of course, but how is profiling an offender different from racially motivated profiling? I think this is the real question. The argument goes back and forth, and there is no clear-cut answer, survey, study, or theory that can pinpoint it. Perhaps, it is up to our fellow police officers to police themselves and have the personal courage to stand up for what is right.

Racial profiling does exist, and I have witnessed it. In the middle 1990s, I changed zones and worked the downtown area, referred to as Zone One. The great thing about being a Zone One PSO in Kalamazoo was that you responded to all fires in the city and were not restricted to patrol only one particular neighborhood—you had the flexibility to roam the entire city. With that, you got "boned" on a lot of calls in other zones, but hey, if you want to be a busy officer then work Zone One.

Zone One was my favorite zone to work. I had a great spot in there in which to do drug interdiction also. The area was what I called "the honey hole." It was at the intersection of the main route to get from the south, east, and north neighborhoods. There was a posted twenty-five–mile-per-hour zone rife with violators. During drug interdiction, the key to success is a numbers game: stop as many cars as possible and try to gain consent or probable cause to search a vehicle. The result is many, many, *many* drug charges.

Working on this plan, I would park perpendicular to the street and keep my headlights on and shining across the street. This position would allow me to see seatbelt violators and items dangling from rearview mirrors. The use of a handheld radar and laser made it perfect to monitor speeding cars coming at me also. Remember, we're talking a numbers game, so that means all traffic violations are going to be stopped regardless of race or gender.

I began to notice a trend about one of my partners, and it took me a good year to catch onto his technique. Perhaps he didn't realize he was doing it, but I did, and it made me suspicious that he was intentionally stopping vehicles with race as a contributing factor in the stop. I saw him let many white offenders, particularly elderly whites, go on their way without being stopped. Not once did a minority get that same treatment. Is that racial profiling? You tell me.

One call we handled together pretty much ended our professional relationship. I responded to a domestic assault call where the relationship was a same-sex, boyfriend/boyfriend assault. It was no different from the typical male/female attacks, just one of the same sex and just as violent. The victim in this case, nicknamed Peaches, had called police for help after he had been assaulted by his live-in boyfriend. The suspect in the case had fled the scene, and I had probable cause to arrest him for domestic violence.

Within minutes after the suspect had fled, my partner contacted me on the radio and advised to me to switch to a tactical channel. While on the other channel, he told me, "Yeah, pretty sure this is your guy. He has the identifiable rainbow tattoo."

I told my partner to just arrest him and handle that part of the case for me while I took care of the victim information. The suspect was subsequently arrested.

Later on that night, we were compiling our reports when I asked my partner if he had the report from that arrest. He replied, "Here's your faggot report."

I was taken aback for a moment and was processing in my mind what to say. Then it just came out. I snapped back, "Thanks, and do you have the nigger reports from earlier, too? I mean, if we're going to bash people, we might as well bash everyone!"

The sergeant's office door burst open, and it was clear that he was pissed. Obviously, he had overheard our conversation (perhaps because I might have been talking loud and in a condescending tone when I snapped back at my partner). I had heard this officer making off-the-wall comments before about gays and minorities, and I was simply fed up with it.

The sergeant ordered, "Todd, go back to the road! You! In my office!"

Nothing else was said to me about this situation. I felt distant from my partner after this incident, and shortly thereafter I switched stations to Zone Six. I felt uncomfortable working with him and felt he could not be trusted. This situation just makes me sick to my stomach.

In an interesting twist of events, since my retirement from Kalamazoo, I had the opportunity to talk to the victim in this case, and Peaches was so proud to tell me that he feels my intervention was fate and that it was the only way he could get out of a violent relationship. He refers to me as his superhero. When I heard that, I said, "You're welcome, Peaches, but I was just doing my job. I'm honored to call you my friend today."

How can we, as a criminal justice profession, address the injustices of racially motivated policing while effectively preventing crime through criminal profiling tactics? The issue is not only racial profiling, but profiling people simply because they are different. So now, this includes everyone, right? And yes, this means white people too. As a society we generally consider race being the only factor when speaking of profiling, when in reality what society is not considering are the totality of circumstances that surround the mind-set of what a police officer is thinking when a potential offender is detained.

I want you to examine this scenario and then ask yourself: Was this a racially motivated police-citizen contact? You are a police officer working in a predominately black neighborhood in an inner-city neighborhood. Your sector of patrol is known for street-level drug deals, and it's commonplace for you to respond to drive-by shootings by which drug dealers are battling each other for turf. The neighborhood is rampant with abandoned homes and run down buildings. Rival gang graffiti is painted all over the street signs, fences, and on the sides of empty buildings. You frequently respond to assaults whereby people walking down the street or sidewalk are attacked and oftentimes robbed. You typically respond to drug overdose medical calls throughout the shift and nearly everyone you come in contact with for either a traffic violation or while on a call are wanted for outstanding warrants. Throughout your tour of duty you are dispatched to citizen complaints of street level drug dealing, loud car stereos, people yelling, and loitering on private property at all hours of the night.

Keep in mind that this is a predominately black neighborhood, and while on patrol you spot a vehicle that has circled the same block three times. As it approaches a group of black males walking alongside the street, it slows down as if the occupants want to say something to them, and then it continues to drive on, but only to drive around the block again. This time it fails to signal a turn. As the car passes, you see the driver is a white male and not wearing a seatbelt. You turn around and immediately stop the car for the observed violations. What questions might come to mind? Remember, you're the police officer. Why is a white guy in this neighborhood? What's your underlying suspicion? What might you suspect this white guy is doing?

He's probably not looking to buy a house, right? No, he's looking to buy drugs. So was this a racially motivated stop? Of course not. First of all, there must be a valid reason to stop a car, i.e., a traffic violation must occur. Simply seeing a white guy driving around may raise your suspicion, but you must develop reasonable suspicion to initiate police contact and/or have a valid reason to detain him, such as any law or ordinance violation.

Now, add one more factor to the above scenario and you can see how we have blurred the racial issue. The police officer is black and the offender is white or visa versa. And in many cases, take this factor out and make the race the same for both. The white offender will assume and proclaim to the officer, "The only reason you stopped me was because I'm a white guy driving in a black neighborhood!"

Let's add one more variable to the above situation. It is the night shift, and you, as the officer, have no idea what the race of the offender may be. But the actions of the vehicle's driver raise your suspicions that criminal activity is afoot. With that, you now have a traffic violation that legally permits you to stop the vehicle. Remember, you have no idea what the race of the driver is.

This is a common issue for every night shift officer that society does not realize or comprehend. Many times, the officer pulling you over, particularly at night, has no idea what your race is, and it does not matter. You're being stopped for the law violation. So, we should not be so quick to blame the officer for stopping people based solely on race.

Another fallacy our society has is this: "Only black people are stopped in this neighborhood," or "Only whites are stopped in this neighborhood." This is especially true in neighborhoods where the majority of the population is made up by one particular race of people. Of course, more whites or blacks are going to be stopped if the make up of the neighborhood is dominated by the particular race. This makes sense, right? It does not mean the officers are racist by any stretch of the imagination.

I hope you can see the difference between criminal profiling and racial profiling. How can issues in profiling people based on anything other than criminal activity be eliminated? I believe it is a matter of education throughout the ranks of all agencies and at every level of an officer's career to help open up a dialogue and method of understanding and mutual respect toward each other as human beings relative not only to race, but also ethnicity, sexual orientation, gender, religious beliefs, and national origin. At the end of the day the issues of police officers focusing attention toward certain individuals or groups must be criminal intent driven and not based on the individual themselves. In addition to education, continued diversification of the police force overall and an active recruiting initiative to seek out qualified minority police officers so that the department maintains a force of highly qualified and educated officers.

PARTY PATROL

Welcome back to Western Michigan University! The first week of September is always a busy time for Kalamazoo Public Safety. The influx of students brings with it a feeling of fun and excitement for new and returning college students. On the other hand, for KDPS officers, especially for Zone Six and Zone One PSOs, it brings with it twelve-hour shifts filled with drunk and obnoxious young adults who relish the prospect of binge drinking, fighting, damaging property, stealing street signs, throwing bottles into the street, setting dumpsters on fire, drunk and drugged driving, and playing loud music that can be heard blocks away until sunrise. These students will argue that Kalamazoo is a college/party town and, therefore, they should be allowed to party. Unfortunately, at its climax of fun and happiness, the party can turn into a full blown riot.

"Party Patrol," as it is known within the department, is an assignment that places officers in specific neighborhoods where the influx of college students takes place and where a pattern of crime develops that is predictable. First, I have to say that party patrol is not about stopping parties or regulating parties in any sense of the word. The term itself describes the mission of the officers assigned to the patrol. The goal is to deter all crimes and to help control the neighborhood disturbances that destroy the quality of life for the residents living in the neighborhoods. Having a party is *not illegal*. What is illegal is the criminal activity that takes place as a result of large crowds that congregate at the party house or apartment.

A party-patrol shift would typically start out around nine in the evening and last until the early morning hours or longer, given the call volume of noise complaints, assaults, fires, or fighting incidents. At the start of the shift, the enforcement aspect usually began with a visible police presence in the given neighborhood through traffic enforcement and foot patrols. As parties were seen to be gathering at a home or apartment, an officer would simply go to the residence and make contact with the tenants or owners and have a casual conversation with the people who were hosting the party.

There were three goals of this conversation. First, it was to let them know that the police were in the neighborhood and to remind them that it's OK to party until people who are not invited start arriving in mass crowds and neighborhood complaints start to get called into dispatch about excessive noise (loud music booming throughout the neighborhood, screaming/yelling, and fighting).

The second goal was to try to build a relationship with the party hosts such that if the party got out of hand they knew they could call the police for help in clearing out those unwanted guests so that their home wasn't pillaged.

The third goal was to remind them, while they were in a not-so-intoxicated state, that the cops were in the area and enforcing the law. We also would let them know that the enforcement, should it take place in regard to the excessive noise ordinance, would result in a ticket or an arrest and there would be no warnings.

In addition to this aspect of community policing we would also water down the many dumpsters in the nearby apartment complexes and nearby fraternity homes as they would become easy targets to set a blaze for the intoxicated reveler looking for late night excitement. You can't start a fire in a dumpster filled with water. But, the unsuspecting couch on the curb takes its place. Our objective in making contact with the partygoers, well before their party got out of hand, was prevention. It is an effective tactic.

Throughout the party-patrol shift it was commonplace for me to issue around twenty appearance and traffic tickets as well arrest an average of one to three people. Multiply these numbers by five to ten PSOs working the patrol, and the total enforcement on a busy night would average eighty tickets and ten arrests.

This activity would also include a multitude of criminal cases being generated: violent/assaultive crimes, rape, simple assaults, home invasions, property damage crime, thefts, resisting/obstructing/fleeing police, fireworks violations, fire code violations, drunk and drugged driving, minor in possession of alcohol, liquor violations, and then finally the quality-of-life crimes: excessive noise (loud music, yelling, disturbing the peace), littering, urinating in public, and disorderly person.

———

On September 9, 2001, we lost a neighborhood. The party-patrol shift started out in typical fashion. However, after I had issued a few appearance tickets for subjects walking down Lafayette Street carrying the familiar red party cup filled with beer, I noticed something was strange about the night. There seemed to be more people than normal milling about. It was warm, though, and the start of a new school year, so it was nothing out of the norm by any means, but it was noticeable. I had a feeling it would be a busy enforcement night. I had no idea the situation would soon turn into a full-blown riot.

I left the neighborhood to make my way back downtown to grab a freshly brewed cup of coffee. I had been out of the neighborhood for only fifteen minutes when I heard screaming over the police radio. "P-One radio, we need more units on Lafayette at Redwood. We're taking bottles!"

I thought, "What the hell? I just left there, and everything was fine." As other officers were responding to the calls for assistance, I anticipated multiple arrests and drove straight to KDPS headquarters to secure the paddy wagon, several bags of flex-cuffs, and my riot helmet. Excellent idea because that's exactly what command requested while I drove away from HQ.

I drove around the area of the melee to Lafayette Street, where I met Sergeant James Ray. As I exited the van, it was struck by exploding beer bottles. There were only a few officers gathered around the intersection to face a mass of thousands of revelers jam-packed in the street and front lawns of the homes in the area. We were completely outnumbered, ill-equipped, and unable to handle the situation. We had lost control. The order was given for all officers to evacuate from the area and regroup elsewhere.

As I was leaving, there were a group of people who approached me. One of them asked, "Where are you going? You have to help us!" I told the group, one of whom was bleeding from the face from an apparent assault, that they should just leave the area. They seemed to be in shock that the cops were leaving.

I told them we'd come back. "When we do, you don't want to be here."

Over the next hour, several officers organized our plan to retake the neighborhood. I was on the SWAT team at the time, so I was reassigned to the SWAT staging area. I donned a backpack full of triple-chaser tear gas grenades and riot gear. Once we organized our team and the other ranks of assisting officers were organized, we began to march back into the neighborhood.

As we approached, we could hear the roar of the crowd and saw an orange glow with smoke emanating from inside the neighborhood. Plain clothes officers were reporting that the crowd had set large fires in the streets and was chanting: "Let's go, Broncos, let's go!" A huge beach ball was being tossed back and forth in the crowd. Also reported were people sitting on roofs, climbing power poles, and hanging from the power lines.

We marched in rank and file, cutting through the back parking lots to bypass the massive crowd. Our plan was to form our skirmish line, march in a line formation to a point where we could launch tear gas, and then push our way into the crowd and disburse the people throughout the neighborhood. This plan would allow the people an escape path out of the area rather than pushing the crowd as a whole toward a swamp and some apartments.

Our team got in a line formation with our largest officers at the front equipped with riot shields and batons. The SWAT officers were behind the main line of shields and were divided into arrest teams. A third file consisted of gas teams and backup arrest officers. Before any type of order to advance on the crowd was given, a lengthy period of verbal warnings over a loud speaker were given to the crowd ordering them to disburse or be arrested for violating an established police line/zone bordered by the nearby streets.

Plain clothes officers within the crowd took control of the beach ball and popped it. This was the spark that made the crowd turn against the police. We were then attacked with a barrage of bottles, rocks, mailboxes, shingles, beer cans full of dirt, fence posts, and lumber set on fire.

"Hold the line! Hold the line! Shields up and forward march!
Stay on line! Stay on line!"

It was difficult to hear the commands being given by the commanders as their voices were drowned out by the deafening roar of the violent crowd we were marching into. Suddenly, I felt an impact on my helmet and was knocked backward. I had just been struck in the head with a forty-ounce glass beer bottle, exploding beer and glass all over me. I regained my footing, wiped my facemask of the beer and continued to move forward with our line. The main line of officers beat their batons against their shields with every other step. Whistles blew, and the command to launch the tear gas was given.

Within throwing range of the main crowd, I hurled multiple triple-chaser tear gas grenades into the rioters. The exploding grenades burst into three pieces of exploding canisters of tear gas. These went spinning through the air, propelling them further into the crowd. With multiple launchings at the same time, the crowd quickly moved and ran for cover. We continued to advance in a line-and-wedge formation, yelling through our gas masks and shining flashlights through the smoke caused by the fires and tear gas. The riot was in full effect now. The barrage of debris, beer bottles, and rocks intensified. The rooftop rioters were above us as we walked down the street, and they were hurling debris from the rooftops down onto us. We had no tactic to repel them other than an overwhelming amount of tear gas to smoke them off the roofs.

I watched as one state trooper was struck in the face and fell down behind a tree. He didn't have his face shield down and was holding his head. Another officer ran to his aid to defend him. Meanwhile, as the main crowd began to run away from us, others were bold. As we came within super-soaker pepper spray range, we dowsed the hostile crowd with streams of it. They continued to curse, scream, and throw rocks, bottles, and anything else they could find to attack us with.

Arrest teams tried to identify the most violent offenders who were close to our ranks throwing rocks and bottles. These violators were targeted and arrested by a group of sprinting officers who burst through our lines to chase them down and arrest them. Our lines continued to move forward and set up additional skirmish lines in front of the arrest teams to protect them as they took the offenders into custody.

In the end, I had thrown seventeen triple-chaser tear gas grenades, was covered in beer and glass, and had been assaulted repeatedly by flying objects. For me, this was a battle! Afterward, once the rioters were disbursed and the neighborhood was secured, it looked like a war zone. The entire area was littered with debris, beer cans, bottles, shingles, uprooted mailboxes, bent over street signs, smashed out windows in parked cars alongside the road, homes damaged with siding hanging off the outside walls, and smoldering debris fires set in the streets.

We took back Lafayette Street, but not without a cost. The very fabric of the neighborhood and our city was damaged. For no reason at all, there was a feeling of hatred toward city government and the police by our young-adult population. This riot, although terrible, would soon fall to the wayside and be replaced by a national tragedy. Just two days later our nation would be attacked on September 11, 2001.

By *The Michigan Daily* on September 9, 2001

KALAMAZOO (AP) A party in a student neighborhood turned violent early yesterday morning, with
revelers damaging cars and other property and
sending two police officers to the hospital, police
said. Kalamazoo Department of Public Safety Lt.

Douglas Geurink said twenty-one people were arrested for charges ranging from inciting a riot to assaulting a police officer. He said forty-six others received citations for underage drinking and other misdemeanors. The disturbance started around midnight Saturday when neighbors complained of noise in a largely student neighborhood, Geurink said. The area "has a history of excessive noise and underage drinking," he said, but has had few problems in recent years. The disturbance wasn't on the campuses of Western Michigan University or Kalamazoo College, which are located nearby. Police estimate about 2,500 people were gathered in the streets when some began damaging street lamps, signs and other public property and set fires in the streets. Kalamazoo Police responded but were pelted with rocks, bottles, sticks and other flying objects. Other agencies were called in, including the Western Michigan University Department of Public Safety, the Kalamazoo County Sheriff's Department and Michigan State Police. About fifty-five officers in riot gear dispersed the crowd with tear gas, Geurink said. "Nobody kind of realized what was going on and all of a sudden comes this wall of riot police spraying Mace and tear gas," Western Michigan student Kevin Wordelman told Grand Rapids television station WOOD-TV. "People were

just running, screaming down the street, terri-
fied. If they didn't have a house to duck into like
we did, I don't know what happened to a lot of the
people that were just stuck out in the street," he
said. Two Kalamazoo police officer s were taken
to Bronson Methodist Hospital, where they were
treated and released for leg and hand injuries.
Geurink said the majority of officers were hit with
objects, but they were protected by helmets and
shields No one else was injured, Geurink said.
Three police cars were damaged, along with other
city and private property, but Geurink said no
cost estimates were available yet. Officers had
the melee under control by about 3:45 a.m., Geurink
said. Police don't know what prompted the disturbance. Police are using videos taken at the scene
to try to identify more suspects. "We are going
to do everything possible to identify those that
broke the law and we will prosecute everyone who
broke law," Geurink said.

Accessed from www.michigandaily.com on Sat, 05 Oct 2013
13:25:43-0400

SPECIAL WEAPONS AND

TACTICS: HOSTAGE RESCUE

In 1993 I passed the selection process and became a member of the Kalamazoo SWAT team assigned to the hostage rescue unit. I served on the team from 1993 to 2002. The training I received within the department and from formal tactical schools was by far the most effective police training I ever had during my career. How does an officer become a member of this elite team? Of course, many new officers and even childhood dreamers fantasize about being on a SWAT team. However, very few officers actually become members of such a force. In Kalamazoo the selection process is based on several factors and continues to evolve as industry standards change and new ideas are inserted into the selection process. Back in 1993, when I was chosen, the selection process consisted of the following:

Any officer who was off probation could submit a memo of interest. This is typically a two-year or more employee. A file review, a physical skills/endurance test, high-stress handgun qualification, scenario-based testing, and a final interview were part of the process.

The file review examines how the prospective SWAT officer has functioned as a street level PSO. SWAT commanders look for officers who are proactive and what we, in the industry would call "ten percenters," that is, those officers who set themselves above the norm by being aggressive. By that I mean nothing abusive, but an officer who seeks out crime before it happens, makes countless arrests, and conducts rock solid investigations. In addition, such an officer is proactive in police/citizen contacts; proactive in traffic law enforcement, drug interdiction, and warrant arrests; and is professional in demeanor when dealing with subjects who are cooperative, potentially uncooperative, and totally uncooperative. This kind of officer is early to work, possesses a great work ethic, seeks self-improvement, seeks department improvement, gives feedback to supervisors on how to make the department a better organization, and holds himself or herself accountable to always do the right thing and to be a leader. Military experience is also considered, but more important is the officer's ability to work as an effective member of a team and be a clear thinker under the most stressful and violent situations.

My nine years with the Kalamazoo SWAT team proved to be a time in my career that I call "tactical transitioning." This is a term I created to describe what happens when an officer transitions from a street cop to a highly trained tactical operator. Officers in this phase have some solid street experience under their belts but then transition into the next phase of their careers in which they become true subject-matter experts in the art of honing their tactical mind-set.

The training with the SWAT team was intense, evolving, demanding, and dangerous, and it blended with my street duties as a public safety officer. It also coincided with the department's efforts to increase tactical patrol training for street officers in addition to creating a new field training program within the agency. The 1990s were a great time for Kalamazoo Public Safety, and I really think this is where the agency became a progressive department with the internal professionalization of many areas of the department. My exposure and expertise, however, were entirely related to patrol. At KDPS we referred to patrol as the Operations Division—"The backbone of the department."

How does a SWAT team train? In Kalamazoo we were granted one day per month to dedicated team training. Each training day was a twelve-hour day that overlapped both day and night. Each month was a different topic taught by different subject matter experts on the team. In addition to in-service training, team members were sent to outside schools across the country to train with other SWAT teams as well as attend nationally recognized seminars such as those offered by the National Tactical Officers Association and West Michigan Tactical Officers Association. This outside training was an excellent concept because it allowed selected officers to attend school and then come back to the department and train our members on any new tactics that were learned. This practice also proved to be highly cost effective and is a *must* for any agency to get the best bang for their buck in regard to training costs. The key, however, is to hold these officers accountable and set aside in-house training sessions to ensure that the training gained is passed on through the ranks of the department. This in-house training proved crucial in the area of hostage rescue for our team and resulted in a higher level of expertise and performance in the area of building entries, room clearing, and hostage rescue tactics.

My nine years on the SWAT team wasn't without incident. Some of my most dangerous and humorous moments took place during SWAT-related activities. As I look back, I know that this intensity was because we all knew that any callout could be our last, and we could fall victim to a suspect's bullet like so many of our comrades have from across the country.

Command to Entry One.
Entry One.
Entry One, move to the entry position. You have control.
Entry One clear on control.
Entry One moving to the entry position.
Command, we are in the entry position.
Entry One, clear you are in the entry position.
Command to Entry One, you have command and control authority.
Entry One clear on command and control.
Entry One, stand by, stand by…initiate, initiate, initiate!
React One to Entry One, S-One is in the kitchen…
shots fired, shots fired, suspect down!

The Knights Inn motel was the scene of two SWAT team moments that had a career-altering effect on me. Each incident, although separate, had similar traits that resulted in both tragedy and victory for our team. One of the great aspects of our chosen profession is that we are quick to learn from past mistakes and are constantly training for and anticipating future events so that they can be handled better than the call before. We are always seeking self-improvement in our actions. The first of such incidents ended in tragedy for the suspect involved.

Two detectives from the Allegan County Sheriff's Department had descended upon the Knights Inn to arrest a subject inside. When the detectives knocked on the door and spoke to the suspect, he indicated that he wasn't coming out and that he would kill the first pig who came through the door. The suspect then fired a gun inside the motel room to express his determination not to go to jail. This shot prompted the detectives to request additional assistance from Kalamazoo Public Safety, which, in turn, resulted in a SWAT team call up to handle a barricaded-subject incident.

The incident started out in the late afternoon hours and continued on into the early morning hours of the next day. One of the benefits a SWAT Team has when dealing with a barricaded subject is time. Time is on our side. Time allows for a tactical team to establish negotiations, conduct reconnaissance, and determine suspect location, mind-set, emotional state, level of aggressiveness, and willingness or unwillingness to surrender. Time also allows for entry teams to rehearse actions upon contact and contingencies prior to making entry. In the case of a motel room, a team is often able to rehearse in an identical motel room that has the same layout and design as the target location. It is nearly a perfect scenario for a tactical team. The great thing about rehearsals is that it takes the guesswork out of the mind of the officers making entry. Rehearse, rehearse, and rehearse. Sometimes, however, there is no rehearsal time, and an emergency entry must be made in active-shooter situations where direct intervention is necessary to save lives and end the violence.

Unfortunately, this wasn't the case in this incident. All of the pieces listed above had been put into place perfectly, yet there is one thing that is always out of your control as a police officer: suspect actions. Officers always try to anticipate suspect actions, but like the weather, we can't control the offensive actions of another human being but can only react to them. Being mindful of the danger cues associated with these actions through our training and experience helps us to acknowledge these danger signs.

I was the first tactical officer through the door after it was breached. As I made entry into the dark motel room, there was only one thought on my mind: "Get to the kitchen!" The flashlight on the end of my MP-5 pierced through the tear gas and flash bang smoke in a narrow beam. Everything seemed to happen at the same time. The suspect looked like a silhouette in my flashlight beam as he dropped to the floor. I don't remember hearing any gunshots; I simply saw his body fall limp to the ground. The suspect had shot himself in the head as the team was making entry. During rehearsals, I had mentally prepared myself for a deadly force encounter and, like any good officer, was looking forward to a good fight. The thought of being shot or killed never crossed my mind and was never an option. I simply convinced myself that the suspect would either surrender or would be firing on me during entry and that I would have perfect shot placement to end the threat.

I had not mentally prepared for option three: the suspect would kill himself before my eyes. When this happened, I felt cheated. "This is not what was supposed to happen!" I thought. We spent all this time preparing to take him into custody or administer deadly force if needed. Suspect suicide was never an option. The entire team felt like we had failed. Most noticeably affected by this tragic turn of events were our hostage negotiators. They had spent hours and hours talking to the suspect, working every angle to convince him to surrender. Suddenly, the person they had spent the hours talking to was dead. They felt terrible, and I was certainly a close second. I think that all of the negative emotions on our faces, although nonverbal, were continuing to build and build inside my mind.

I found myself second-guessing my own actions and that of our team. Did we do everything possible to prevent this death? Was there something we could have done differently that would have resulted in a living apprehension? I found that I was actually blaming myself for his death.

The day following the incident, we conducted our critical incident stress debriefing. As the debriefing began, I felt myself getting hot and feeling flushed just sitting in a circle of chairs with other officers. All the officers explained their roles in the incident and how they felt. The department psychologist was present and asked some really pointed questions. When the debriefing began, it seemed like nobody was affected by the situation. "Was I the only one?" I thought, or were the guys just being too manly about the situation? I felt my heart racing and my palms sweating as my turn was fast approaching.

I leaned forward in my chair with my hands on my knees and said, "I feel like shit." I told the group that I was blaming myself for the suspect's death. I couldn't put into words why I felt this way, but I remember telling them that I trained and prepared for every option except for the suspect killing himself. I felt that if I had also considered this as an option, I would not be experiencing the posttraumatic stress that I was now shouldering. When the inspector and the psychologist inquired, I said I didn't think the incident would hinder my ability to continue working my shift, I just felt like I needed to express my emotions because they were tearing me up inside.

My voice cracked, and I forced myself to hold back the tears, but I really just felt like shit inside. This incident continued to bother me for a good six months before I was convinced that it wasn't my personal actions that caused the suspect to kill himself and that he made that decision when he put the gun to his head and pulled the trigger. My partners were the best healers I could have had. Many of them would ask if I was doing OK and would give me a pat of reassurance on the back. They told me I did a great job on the scene. This was the best therapy I could have had—the assurance from my teammates that I did the right thing and nothing was my fault. The camaraderie of our team was unbreakable, and it was this bond in battle that kept us strong and developed us into a great force of good. The end goal in any situation is for the suspect to be apprehended with no injuries to officers, civilians, or the suspect.

Entry One Command, we are in the entry position.
Entry One, you have command and control.
Clear on that, Command. Entry one has control.
Entry One, breacher up!
Standby, Standby, Standby…Initiate, Initiate, Initiate!

An incident with a second barricaded subject at the Knights Inn took place later during this same year. Ironically, it was on the same floor and only three rooms away from the first tragedy. This incident, however, ended with a more preferred outcome. The suspect was arrested without injury.

The incident started out as public safety officers were dispatched to the Knights Inn motel after a report of a subject screaming and yelling. As the officer knocked on the door, the subject opened up the door slowly, and then reached through the door opening with a knife and tried to stab the officer. The officer slammed the door shut and requested back up. The incident resulted in a barricaded subject armed with a knife and wanted for felonious assault against a police officer.

The incident had similar traits to our previous barricaded-gunman call. The SWAT team again conducted extensive rehearsals using an identical motel room for practice. Meanwhile a react team was in position and negotiators were attempting to make contact with the suspect. This time, though, negotiators made no contact, so the intelligence that would normally be gained through verbal negotiations with the suspect wasn't known.

The waiting time came to a quick end. Only a few hours had gone by when the decision to send in the entry team was made. There was an interesting twist, though, to the command decision on whether or not to make entry or to continue ongoing efforts to establish subject contact. I had the occasion to be present in the command center during the decision-making process by the Chief of Public Safety and his other top commanders. The process was not like anything I had seen before. Essentially the decision to allow the SWAT team to make entry was the chief's responsibility. I watched as the chief asked each of his commanders about his or her personal thoughts on what should be done. All but one commander insisted that entry be made.

One, however, said, "I'll pass."

The chief said, "You can't pass! Tell me what you think!"

The underlying issue was that each commander in the room knew that if the SWAT team made entry and was confronted by a knife-wielding suspect that deadly force would surely be administered. The entry team had other options in mind. In our minds we knew we were dealing with an emotionally deranged person (EDP), as cops refer to them. We knew that there was a chance that the suspect could be incapacitated with high-pressure aerosol spray and deadly force may not be needed.

The chief made the decision: "Make entry and get this thing over with!"

The breacher smashed down the door, multiple flash bangs were deployed, and I made entry through the doorway. My focus was directed to the suspect's hands. "No knife," I thought. The suspect ran toward the bathroom door, but he was doused in pepper spray and instantly pushed to the ground and handcuffed. The suspect wasn't armed.

Mission success! This was one of those high-five moments that the public does not see. After the room was checked for any additional suspects, our team left the room and redeployed to our staging area. The balaclavas and helmets were peeled off our heads and faces, weapons were placed on safety, and entry vests were peeled off our sweat-soaked bodies, and the high-fives and celebratory hand slaps took place. We were on cloud nine.

Did we want to take a life that day? Hell, no! Were we prepared to do so? Hell, yes! As officers, our fundamental duty is to serve and protect. The successful apprehension of any violent offender is our ultimate goal.

"Radio Zone Three, start for Horace Avenue. A male subject called
nine-one-one
reporting he had just cut his wife's throat."

At six thirty in the morning, the shift responded to this nine-one-one call. Normally at that time officers are conducting shift change procedures, finishing their workouts, peeling themselves out of the station La-Z-Boy chairs, and drinking fresh coffee while catching up on the gossip of the day. This call was *not* how we wanted to end or begin our shift, and I was exhausted from having worked the entire night. This was the last thing I wanted to deal with, but duty called.

When officers made contact at the home, they found a female lying on the front porch. She had bled severely from the neck and died. The male suspect who called nine-one-one remained inside the home and was refusing to come out. The call resulted in another SWAT call-up for a barricaded subject.

This call, however, was fast-paced and over within just a few hours. I arrived on scene and reported to the command post. I was quickly assigned to the react team and sent to a staging area adjacent to the front porch of the home. The suspect inside was threatening to burn down the house and kill himself.

Shortly after meeting up with my partners, I noticed that other PSOs had been put into fire suppression positions next to us by the house. Meanwhile, a second react team took up a position at the rear of the home that also had an attached garage. While both our teams were taking up our positions, light smoke began to emit from underneath the eaves of the house, and flames could be seen inside through the front window. The suspect carried out his threats and set his own house on fire while inside.

This development created a flurry of activity on the scene and chatter over our SWAT radio system. Command had directed both react teams to make an emergency entry with the fire suppression team. This was a challenge our team had never faced. The issue at hand was to protect the fire suppression team while making an emergency entry to apprehend the suspect.

I took up a new position at the rear of the home with the entry team while the fire suppression team was told to hold its position. Our intent was to make entry at the back of the home and apprehend the suspect before the fire spread out of control. Contrary to any type of fire suppression operation, our SWAT team was to make entry into a smoke-filled structure with a rapidly spreading fire in an effort to essentially conduct a search and rescue of an armed and dangerous murder suspect.

At the garage area near the back of the home, the entry team began its assault. Multiple pepper spray canisters and flash bangs were simultaneously deployed into each window while the entry team breached the back door. The front react team and fire suppression team were ordered to hold their positions until a search for the suspect could be conducted.

I remember entering the garage area, which was filled with pepper spray gas and flash bang smoke, and the air was filling rapidly with choking house fire smoke. There was a significant temperature change inside the home, because the fire in the front of the house was spreading rapidly.

"Suspect down! Suspect down!" I yelled out as our team located the suspect in a corner of the smoke-filled garage. He was completely naked and covered in an oily substance and looked bloated and puffy for some reason. He was taken into custody as our team leader directed the react team to enter the front of the building and provide security to the initial fire attack team.

There was no rehearsal for this incident. We simply reacted to the circumstances at hand. Later in the afternoon, I learned that the suspect died at the hospital that same day. I was shocked, and his death made no sense to me. My first thoughts were that he died from the smoke or pepper spray inhalation, but it was determined that he actually died from a drug overdose.

In Kalamazoo, we are fortunate to all be cross-trained as both police officers and firefighters. We knew that the officers on the nozzle were also cops who were not afraid to face a suspect's bullet. In turn, they trusted their lives to their armed SWAT partners who would protect them during the initial fire attack had they confronted the suspect in an armed confrontation. Unfortunately, for many agencies, this is not the case. When was the last time your police department conducted joint training with the firefighters of your area? Calls like the one just described are certainly not unique. Although rare, during dangerous situations, particularly involving barricaded subjects, there is a fire danger present.

TACTICAL ASPECTS INCLUDE:

1. Negotiations
2. Surveillance
3. Establishment of a "React Team"
4. Evacuations of bystanders in proximately to the target location to ensure the safety of the nearby public
5. Traffic control
6. Establishment of media safe zones
7. Entry Team Rehearsals
   - Staging locations
   - Entry positions
   - Chemical agent deployment
   - Breaching procedures

- Actions upon entry
- Actions upon suspect contact
- Room clearing tactics
- Officer-down drills
- Deadly force encounter
- Multiple suspects/hostages
- Barricaded entry points and alternate entry points
- Rouse/Distraction techniques

8. Actions upon surrender
9. Actions for emergency entry (react team responsibility)
10. SWAT sniper positioning/spotters
11. Search warrant/arrest warrant procurement
12. Tactical EMS/fire support
13. Hospital ER notification
14. Evacuation procedures
15. Food/Rest plans for officers

I decided to write about only the most memorable SWAT calls I had. Our team was an on-call SWAT team made up of highly trained tactical officers who spent the remainder of their duty days at their assigned positions throughout the department. When a call up would take place, each officer was pager notified and would respond according to the emergency at hand. As I look back at my nine years on the team, I am proud to see the accomplishments that I had as an individual member of the organization. It was an honor to serve with these professional officers, and I take great pleasure in being able to look back at my SWAT team days and know that I helped make the team a better unit than when I was selected to become a member. During my tenure on the team, I worked to create the "SWAT medic" program with the local medical control and Life EMS Ambulance service and helped develop and instruct the first "mobile active shooter" training program in Kalamazoo County. I certainly appreciate the opportunity I was given by Kalamazoo Public Safety to be a member of this amazing team.

Among all of these memorable SWAT calls, what else happens? Training, training, and more training. With any battle-hardened team comes the brotherhood and camaraderie associated with the team concept. Some of my most comedic and memorable events were not dealing with the public, but dealing with my fellow officers. You just can't make this stuff up.

Imagine a fully loaded, breadbox style van of SWAT officers set to pull out of the back of the training division with a new SWAT officer at the wheel. We were ready to execute a search warrant and had our heart rates up, equipment checked, radios programmed, weapons loaded, and minds all focused on the mission at hand. The van's engine started up and the vehicle made a violent leap forward, crashing head on into the AT&T Telephone building adjacent to the parking lot. Officers were piled up on the floor, into the doorway, and against the front glass. Amid the cursing, laughing, and utter chaos of officers lying on top of each other, bullets scattered about the floor, gear and helmets flying through the air, one voice rang out: "Hey, don't start the van with it in gear!"

On another occasion, the SWAT team was traveling to a high-risk drug raid to execute a search warrant. Intelligence suggested that the suspects were armed and dangerous and were smuggling drugs from Detroit to Kalamazoo. Kalamazoo SWAT was on the way. The van was quiet as we were all listening to the eye update command on movement at the house. Another new SWAT officer was at the wheel of the van. As we approached an intersection, the van suddenly came to an abrupt stop.

Eight SWAT officers who were all standing up in the van holding onto the bars above, sweat running down our brows from the lack of air conditioning, went flying forward into a pile near the driver at the front of the van. The smooth voice of Officer Kelvin Oliver spoke up out of the pile: "Next time, just run the light!" Then the laughter began, as we slowly peeled ourselves off one another from our heap of ballistic vests, helmets, and MP5 submachine guns. We retook our positions and prepared to continue on with our mission. I think I actually made entry into the house still laughing from the event. As the point man on the entry team, I was lucky enough to be at the back of the van and be on the top of this "pig pile" of cops.

POLICE TRAINING CAN BE JUST AS DEADLY AS DEALING WITH SUSPECTS

How do officers get shot during training or by accident? As cops we are handling guns on a daily basis, be it our own or that of a suspect. The problem with cops is that we think we know what we're doing with firearms because we're used to handling them so much. The act of handling a weapon actually becomes routine. *Routine* is one of the worst words in the law enforcement profession. There is nothing routine about handling weapons, just as there should not be anything routine about dealing with the public at any level. Many such gun incidents come to mind as I look back in my career. Every incident dealt with carelessness on the part of the officer involved.

My first near-miss incident took place during SWAT training when we were practicing vehicle assaults. The scenario was a suspect about to go mobile in a vehicle with a hostage. The hostage rescue team made its approach to the suspect vehicle simultaneously with SWAT snipers, who initiated fire along with the deployment of distraction devices on the hood of the vehicle.

During our training, my team made its approach, and the suspect was identified as the figure sitting in the driver's seat. As I made my approach along the driver's side of the car, my adrenaline got the best of me, and I pushed my handgun forward to the mannequin suspect's head for a close head shot while other officers were firing through the back window at the driver's head. Screaming in the background was the SWAT commander: "Cease fire! Cease fire!" Of course nobody could hear him when the triggers were being pulled. The assault completed, the commander brought to my attention that both of my hands were inside the suspect vehicle while firing. Fortunately for me, the headrest of the driver seat soaked up the nine millimeter rounds being fired through the back windows, and my hands were not shot off! Note to self: "When making a head shot to a suspect and other officers are shooting into the car, don't put your hands inside the car!

ASSUME EVERY WEAPON IS LOADED AND NEVER BECOME COMPLACENT

Horseplay! Absolutely not permitted, but within our SWAT ranks it happened. I was in the back of the van returning to the station after day-long hostage rescue training when bad turned worse. Horseplay is the only way to describe what happened. One officer had loaded his handgun and placed it back into his thigh holster while another officer unholstered this same weapon to demonstrate some sort of ridiculous act of courage and pulled the trigger. Thank God the only damage was to the floor of the van. The look on the face of the officer who pulled the trigger went from laughter to shock when the gunshot rang out inside the van. We could not believe what had just happened, and we felt our bodies to see if we had been shot. This completely ruined the training day and resulted in severe disciplinary action.

High-risk drug search warrants always stressed me out the most. I think the buildup of anticipation and fear of the unknown were contributing factors to this anxiety. The sequence of events was as follows:

- It all started when the pager went off.
- Then there was the drive into the station, getting dressed, grabbing the gear pack, and checking weapons.
- This was followed by the intelligence briefings, where you were locked in the briefing room with no phone use.
- Then came the dry-run rehearsals on actions upon entry and actions upon contact, with officer-down drills and deadly force drills.
- Added to the preparations were map overlays, and a review of photos, suspect pedigree and past history of violence, and suspected weapons and barricades.
- Officers would do deep breathing to try to stay cool under the heavy body armor. There was a constant build up of anxiety to the van ride.
- We were all thinking of contingencies and "what ifs." What if I get hit? What will I do? What if my partner gets shot? What will I do?
- It all comes to a moment of climax when the first flash bangs are deployed. Then rooms are cleared and suspects are taken into custody, followed by primary-secondary searches, weapons safety checks, and then a reload back to the van. The

adrenaline dump happens during the ride back to the station. I've even seen guys fall asleep heading back to the station. That's all as a result of the adrenaline dump, the drop in heart rate and blood pressure, and a sigh of relief.

As a tactical officer, you must remove all aspects associated with fear. Use this feeling of anticipation as a strength to continue on with the mission. If not, it will consume you. You must not think about anything but victory and mission completion—no matter what! Even if shots are fired, the mission continues.

Something I wish I could have been told as a SWAT officer was something that one of my best friends, Keaton Nielsen, told me as we made final approach into Kabul, Afghanistan, on a C-17 transport plane on deployment in 2009. The feeling was tense as we were preparing to land in a combat zone. Keaton, who was sitting next to me in the plane, leaned over and yelled out, "Just consider yourself dead, and you'll do just fine!" This made complete and total sense to me. All aspects of reality and life were out of my hands and simply in the control of my surroundings. I had to survive and thrive in this hell if I was to ever make it out of here alive. You can't think about the possibility of getting killed. You must think of just winning/surviving and doing the job at hand. I'll talk more about Officer Keaton Nielsen later as he proved to be one of the most influential people in my life and still is to this day.

STUPID SHIT I DID AT WORK

GUNFIRE IN THE EVIDENCE ROOM

How I didn't get shot in the evidence room in 2008 is amazing. I had taken a Kimber forty-five caliber gun off a Chicago-based gang member after a man-with-a-gun call. While placing the bullets that I removed from the weapon into the evidence locker, I accidentally dropped the manila envelope of loose rounds. As the envelope hit the ground, each and every round went off at my feet, disintegrating the envelope, filling the room with gun smoke, and leaving numerous ricochet marks on the floor and walls. How I didn't get shot was a miracle. My guardian angels were looking out for me that day. I felt my legs for bullet holes and blood and waited for the hot rush to hit me. I was in complete disarray with burning bits of envelope all over my uniform and in my hair.

Lieutenant Lenkart had heard or seen the gunfire and came through the door. "Are you OK?" he said. I told him, "They just blew up."

PEPPER SPRAY, ANYONE? SWAT TRAINING, FORT CUSTER, MICHIGAN

The trainer had brought some brand new pepper spray. "Who wants to test it?" he asked.

I said, "Hooah! I'll do it!"

Boy, was that a stupid idea. I took a face full of pepper spray, and the pain was incredible. I literally took off running into the woods and was trying to find a stick to impale myself upon. That's what the pure panic of my first encounter with pepper spray did to me. An hour later, after riding on the hood of the training suburban driving up and down the range road, I finally found some small relief. The moving vehicle was the only wind that could be generated on a hot summer day. Pain, pain, and more pain! The pepper spray remnants of pain last for hours.

This action was stupid. But, hell, we all had to take a shot, and looking back, it surely helped me in real-world environments as I was pepper sprayed two more times while taking suspects into custody. With each incident, you become more immune to the effects of the spray and can fight through the pain to get the job done. All officers need to experience the pain of their own less-lethal weapon systems so that if they're exposed, or these weapons are used against them, they're not taken off guard. They know how it feels and can fight through the pain to make an arrest. They have personal knowledge of the effects on other people. So, it wasn't stupid. It was a great training episode. All officers should experience a face full of pepper spray during training so they can fight through it when it happens to them on the street and can properly decontaminate their suspects who experience the same pain.

One time that I was sprayed in the face occurred when my partner tried to stop a juvenile suspect who was kicking out the back windows of the patrol car. It happened again after I arrested a suspect for retail fraud at a liquor store when he decided he wasn't going to jail and tried to flee from me. Well, that pepper spray not only found its way directly into the face of the suspect, but did a perfect rebound right back into my eyes. Fight through the pain! Hell, I heard my own voice yelling at myself as I struggled to regain control of the suspect.

CHOKING ON FRENCH FRIES

A wonderful night of overtime party patrol nearly ended with me choking to death at Station Six. Officer Gary Gaudard and I wheeled into the station for a quick break, and what did I spot on the stove? Freshly cooked french fries of the best kind: from a firefighter! I took a leak, refilled my coffee, scooped up a handful of the wonderful delights, and headed out the front door toward our patrol car. I shoveled a handful of fries into my mouth. They clearly had no intention of going into my stomach, but rather my lungs. These were not your soft, chewy fries either. Oh no, they were the hard and crispy type.

With complete blockage of my airway, I dropped my coffee on the ground and ran to the driver's side door, opened it, and rolled down the window. Flinging my body through the opening of the window I slammed my abdomen down onto the edge of the door and out flew the hard french fries onto the ground. In a panic I looked at Gary, who was reading a newspaper and glaring at me over his glasses.

He asked, "Are you all right?"

I said, "Gary, I was choking. I could have died."

Gary, in his quick wit, replied, "Jesus, man! Well, don't die. We have tickets to write and people to arrest." With that, I sat back down, wiped the tears out of my eyes, began laughing, and away we went to ruin someone's day.

NEARLY CRASHING INTO AND KILLING MY PARTNER

Sweet Waters donut shop was a popular hangout for a midnight shift PSO to grab a cup of coffee. Yes, and a donut! I was field training with Officer Karen Rivard. We met up with Officer Chuck Dahlinger and decided to drive to Sweet Waters to grab a cup of coffee and take our twenty-minute break away from the realities of life. For whatever stupid reason, Chuck and I decided it would be a great time to fly down the street in our 1992 Chevrolet Caprice cruisers, powered by a Corvette-type engine. Yes, I'm sure we were speeding. Chuck, being the traffic enforcement guru that he was, just couldn't resist the one-headlight violator that was approaching him. I had been following closely behind Chuck as we sped along, and I was distracted as I talked to my rookie officer next to me, explaining to her the finer things of life. Chuck decided to pull a U-turn directly in front of me, but his idea of a U-turn was to veer to the right and then make a sharp left turn, since he had four lanes to maneuver in. Well, not such a good idea when there was a distracted driver (me) right behind him. In an instant, I saw Chuck's body sideways in front of my headlights as I was speeding toward his driver's door. I managed a quick jerk of my steering wheel to the right with no brakes and a counter steer back to the left followed by a hard brake. Jesus Christ, how the hell I didn't kill him I'll never know.

We turned around slowly and pulled in behind Chuck on his traffic stop. "Chuck, I almost killed you. Holy fuck!"

With a Chuck Dahlinger laugh he replied, "Nah, I saw you. You were good."

Well, off to coffee we went.

NEAR RIOT SITUATION AND CAUSING A PERSONAL INJURY ACCIDENT

Kalamazoo officers are commonly tasked with doing ride-alongs with citizens who want to see what it's like as a Kalamazoo cop on patrol. Many officers hated to take ride-alongs, but I loved to show off our department. One ride-along sticks in my mind as one of the funniest moments of my career. Well, it wasn't that funny at the time, but it was pretty ironic.

Back in the middle 1990s, the City of Kalamazoo came up with an initiative called something like "Reducing the Cost of Governmental Services." Many of these ideas came from city employees. Well, I had a ride-along from an insurance agent who was examining ways the city could save tax dollars in public safety.

While on patrol, a large fight broke out at a nightclub known as Nancy's Place. The fight involved several people. Many officers were calling for backup because rocks and bottles were being thrown at the police. I was in a hurry to get on scene. At one intersection, I stopped and looked to the north for oncoming traffic. I saw nothing coming; however, a large Consumers Energy truck was parked in the street and blocking my view. As I pulled out, I smashed into the side of a passing car and caused the other car to flip over sideways into the intersection, adding total panic to an already out-of-control situation. Right after I hit the car, I looked at my ride-along to see if he was OK. I said, "Well, there's one thing we can do to save money."

"How's that?" he said, as he brushed the glass out of his hair.

"By not crashing into people!" I said.

I got a ticket for the accident, per our policy. Luckily for me, though, I fought the ticket in court and was found not responsible by the magistrate. Basically, I was responding to an emergency, with emergency lights and siren activated, and due to the Consumers Energy truck blocking my view, I was found not responsible. If I had been found responsible, though, I would have paid the fine.

FAILURE TO PAY ATTENTION TO DETAIL
KDPS was no joke when it came to any inkling of potential dishonesty, and this was an excellent policy. Being fired for dishonesty in my book is

perfectly acceptable. Unions may have something else to say about that, but for the most part I'm sure many officers would agree that personal integrity is paramount. I fell victim to two such incidents, by my own lack of attention to detail that were interpreted by the investigating command officer as being a form of dishonesty when, in fact, they were simple mistakes. Still, public safety officers are held to a higher standard than your average human being. I completely take responsibility for these two situations and hope that other officers who read this will learn from my mistakes.

My first suspension was due to my questioning of a shift lieutenant and putting the wrong date for my grandfather's funeral on a memo. As the lieutenant was lecturing me about the disciplinary action I would be facing it reminded me of a quote I recalled from the Army: "Don't confuse your rank with my authority." I had submitted a memo and a copy of the obituary to dispute sick time that was taken from my sick time bank. Well, on the first memo I submitted for time off, I had put the wrong date for the funeral. Then I contradicted myself on the second memo when I appealed the deduction of sick time to attend the funeral. The captain granted me the sick time, but it was my shift lieutenant who felt that my questioning was out of line. I was slapped with an accusation of lying to a command officer. The discipline resulted in a one-day suspension without pay. I guess they got their sick time back. I always wondered if the lieutenant felt they made the right decision by launching the accusation that I was being deceptive, when in fact, the underlying theme to counter my appeal was that I was granted the sick time back from the captain. Regardless, I should have simply paid closer attention to detail.

The second suspension came as a result of another clerical mistake. This time, I was taking comp time when there really was no time to take off. This was a big one: a fifteen-day suspension, which is one month's pay!

After several different interviews by internal affairs and a different line of interrogating, I just got so sick of it. I told the investigator, "Look, just fire me, but I'm not admitting to lying, because I didn't lie!" Needless to say, they must not have had enough to fire me, and they nailed me to the wall with the suspension and a transfer back to patrol from the community policing unit. I'm certainly not bitter about these situations, but I can see how an innocent person can be found responsible for something he or she did not do. Again, though, it was a failure to pay attention to detail on my part.

There are always good things that come out of mistakes, and I try to find the positives rather than the negatives in my life and at work. In both situations, knowing that I was found guilty by the agency, I still didn't let this negative energy affect my work ethic. I continued to do my job at the same level that I always have, even after being wronged. I didn't throw my sucker in the dirt and pout like many have done; instead, I just did my job as I was expected to do it. You see, in my mind that is what they wanted me to do: to become a burden and a nonperformer. Not a chance. Not Officer Todd. No way. Why? Because I'm a winner not a loser!

In time, the policy and procedures on how to take time off and the tracking of that system changed to make it virtually impossible for anyone to screw up, and for that matter, be wrongfully accused. So, I would say that my situation paved the way for a better working environment and a better system than just a pen and a memo pad. In the end, though, my suggestion is to *pay attention to detail*. I could have easily avoided both situations had I paid closer attention to detail.

I'm very proud to say that I was never disciplined for poor treatment of any citizen or in the performance of my duties of a public safety officer. My mistakes and discipline came from administrative errors on my part, not those affecting the general public and my community. I'll take that as a career victory any day!

> *"Always remember who you are and what you represent."*
> *Jeff Shouldice, College Professor*

As I look back over my career, I think about the officers I worked with who were fired, investigated, disciplined, arrested, or who took their own lives. Believe it or not, police officers are simply human beings. We all have our own personal issues and complications, but when you add the fact that police officers are entrusted to ensure public safety, our level of personal conduct both on and off duty is seen through a more exact lens of moral and ethical expectations. However, as I revisit what these officers did, I can see a pattern of behavior or a trend that may have played a role in their less-than-professional decisions. The interesting thing about the law enforcement profession is that it is a glorified career and one that carries with it a higher level of responsibility and expectations that revolve around trust. My intent is that, as you read what these officers did, you can learn from them and monitor your own personal conduct to avoid bringing embarrassment to the law enforcement profession. Remember, *you* represent the communities you serve.

- A dispatcher sees an alert for a recovered crossbow from another agency. The information came to him from the LEIN system (Law Enforcement Information Network). He then makes contact with the original agency reporting falsely that he was the owner of the crossbow in question and attempts to gain possession of the item.

- An officer uses department memo paper to write down his name and personal phone number to give to a prostitute with the intent to purchase crack cocaine and sexual acts. This same memo is later found in the prostitute's personal property when she's arrested on an unrelated prostitution charge. An investigation reveals this officer is a drug user and prostitution offender.

- A command officer flees from the department when he is questioned about having keys to the evidence room and is suspected of stealing drugs. He is pursued by other officers and arrested. This same officer was also a suspect in pimping out prostitutes and providing them with crack cocaine.

- An officer who is working in dispatch takes a noncriminal complaint from a citizen who wants to turn in a handgun he found. When the officer is finished working dispatch, he responds to the address of the person who originally called police to report the found gun, and the officer takes the weapon. The problem is, the officer does not complete the investigation and decides to keep the weapon for himself. Months later the reporting citizen contacts public safety in an effort to retrieve the found gun, but it's nowhere to be found in evidence. An investigation reveals the officer never turned in the weapon but kept it.

- A retired firefighter is arrested and charged with drunk driving, and multiple other offenses. The retiree kills himself by gunshot in a field behind his home.

- An officer is facing criminal sexual assault charges and takes his own life in the basement of the police station.

- Officers are arrested for drunk driving while off duty.
- An officer falsifies the comp time tracking book and then submits for comp time that never existed in the form of additional pay.
- An officer is disciplined for lying during courtroom testimony.
- An officer lies about working overtime to gain more pay.
- A new hire is fired shortly after he is hired for lying on his employment application about his driving record.
- An officer lies about breaking department property and is fired.
- A firefighter is fired for smoking marijuana while on duty.
- An officer is fired/resigned for failing to take a drug test when ordered.
- An officer is fired and charged criminally for purchasing drugs from undercover officers.

I listed just a few examples of actual events that took place while I was employed with Kalamazoo Public Safety. I know there are many, many more incidents where officers were disciplined, fired, and charged criminally for the acts they committed. It is not my intent to bring embarrassment to our profession, since these incidents and many more are publicly known, and you can easily research similar incidents on your own. My intent is to get a point across to my fellow officers and those who aspire to become police officers. Do you see a pattern? Drugs, alcohol, money/financial/personal gain, sex, lying.

When or if you find yourself considering acts that are criminal or unethical in nature, simply don't do it, but if you cannot control these evil thoughts then please, for the sake of our profession, please resign. In the end, you will be caught, and your life will be ruined. I applaud our Office of Professional Standards and am comforted to know that within our agency there is a network of officers who police the agency. Our community deserves the best public servants our society has to offer.

FIELD TRAINING AND
ROOKIES

"Let no soul cry out, Had I been properly trained."
Infantry Training Brigade, Fort Benning, Georgia

D ay-one new kids are commonly greeted as "Hey, new kid!" in the briefing room. Here they come, thirty minutes early to work. New uniforms, crispy shoulder patches, bright leather gun belts, and gear bags full of manuals, pens, and all the new trinkets and gadgets these new kids can spend their money on.

"You know why I don't call you by your name yet, new kid? Because you could be dead in twelve hours, and I don't want to be emotionally attached to you." It was common for most veteran officers to greet a rookie officer in this manner. Now, that's a great way to start a shift, right? I thought so. Next stop, the Davis Street hill on the East Campus of Western Michigan University overlooking all of downtown Kalamazoo.

"Baker 11 City, show 11 and 11A out of service for training."

I took the job as a Field Training Officer in 1993. I considered it the most important position within my agency. An FTO is the sole officer personally responsible for setting the standard and helping to mentor and train the future of our department.

"Take off your collar brass."

"What?"

"Yes, hand over your collar brass. You have to earn that." I started this tradition late in my FTO career, and I wish I'd done it to every new kid I trained. I did this only in phase one of the FTO program. Upon completion of phase one, we held a collar-brass-pinning ceremony at the flag pole as a rite of passage from phase one to phase two.

Now for my secret conversation never revealed to the public that took place between myself and a new officer I was training. Overlooking the city of Kalamazoo, I would explain to the new kid that over the next twenty-five years he or she would give a full commitment to this city and dedicate his or her life, and potentially give it, to defend the very people down there as we looked down the hill and over the city skyline.

I would tell new officers that it was this very city that would pay for their next car, house mortgage, their kids' braces, new clothes, tennis shoes, health care, and college tuition—that they would owe their entire life and future to the city of Kalamazoo and, in the end, it would be this very city that would pay for their livelihood into retirement. So, what does this mean to us as public safety officers? It means full, total, and unbridled dedication and commitment to the citizens who are entrusting us with their lives, protection, and service. At all costs, no matter what, we are to always put the citizens before ourselves and serve them at all times. *We are the city of Kalamazoo*, and never forget that!

I would also tell them that it's OK to have friends on the department. We are a family. We are all here for each other and to help each other every day, but don't get too attached to these people. You always have to keep in mind that at any moment your best friend could be gunned down, hit by a car or train, dragged from a vehicle, beaten to death, or burned up in a fire. Then guess what? You still have to come to work the next day, you still have to sit through briefing while looking at an empty chair, and you still will be expected to go throw on your vest, strap on your gun belt, get in your car, and go back out there and fight crime and fire, save lives, and take the calls. So don't get too attached. You have to be a brother or a sister and still have the mental strength to accept the reality that death is possible here. Remember that!

TRAINING THE FORCE—THE FIELD TRAINING OFFICER PROGRAM

In this section, I'm going to explain how the field training officer program works and how we strived as an agency to improve upon our program. It's my intention that others will read this section and take pieces of the program and help make their own field training program a success within your agency. Of all things important to me, training our new officers was by far the most sacred honor I ever had as a Kalamazoo public safety officer.

Economic challenges facing police agencies throughout the country have not deterred one Michigan police agency from continuing to deliver a superior field training officer program. The Kalamazoo Department of Public Safety, like many agencies in the country, has faced difficult financial realities while maintaining essential services and streamlining service delivery. It was a matter of "creating a more lean and efficient model of public safety," as Chief Jeff Hadley put it. Kalamazoo Public Safety recognized this challenge and aggressively answered the call by embracing an innovative approach to training. The department sought to perfect the professional by identifying subject matter experts within the organization to deliver top-notch training based on perceived organizational needs. This mind-set resulted in more effective, reality-based training that drew from existing internal resources without sacrificing quality.

ORGANIZATIONAL HISTORY AND FIELD TRAINING OFFICER TRAINING

At Kalamazoo Public Safety, the modern-day field training officer training program, Train the Trainer, has evolved since its inception in the 1990s. Prior to that, there was no standard for field training of new hires. The original program normally consisted of a two-week ride-along that could be described as a familiarization of the patrol process. A new officer would merely ride with an experienced officer from his or her precinct until the new officer felt comfortable enough to work in solo patrol. Often, there was no accountability of training or documentation of the behavior or actions of the new hire. Before the new officers arrived for the two-week tour of duty, they had already attended an advanced police academy and had become a certified Michigan police officer and firefighter. Officers were exposed to the internal operations, policies and procedures, and updates on specified aspects of criminal law. Rarely did the two-week tour of duty represent what we now know as "field training."

KDPS field training officers have embraced the basic FTO model while continually updating training modules and evaluations that focus on the police, firefighting, and emergency medical services disciplines. In

Kalamazoo, the field training process has evolved over time and continues to change and be improved upon as new challenges occur.

Recently, one of the major issues was the lack of funding to send officers to outside FTO schools for a weeklong training course. As a result of the dilemma, the agency looked internally to find qualified instructors, as well as subject matter experts, who could coordinate and conduct an in-service Field Training Officer course that would satisfy the training needs of the department while simultaneously reducing the cost of attending outside schools. This process, which began in 2005, resulted in a more internal Field Training Officer training model.

A basic problem in previous years of training field training officers was that the external training appeared generic and inapplicable to the specific needs of Kalamazoo Public Safety. Routinely, field trainers who had attended such courses expressed concern that the specific needs of KDPS were not met with a cookie-cutter training program. Additionally, materials used in such external training courses were seldom up-to-date with modern police practices, especially those used by KDPS, which required field training officers to be multidisciplinary. Cost was also an issue, as the 2008 recession added another dimension to the frustration of attending inapplicable external training.

IDENTIFYING THE INTERNAL EXPERTS TO TRAIN

As the frustration mounted, KDPS administration targeted the problem by determining who would be the most effective instructor to facilitate the training of FTOs within the agency. Identifying these experts required leaders to know their people when making such decisions. This process occurred largely by instinct, but discussions about teaching abilities, instructor experience, subject knowledge, patrol experience, credibility among peers, and out-of-agency professional experience were needed. Military experience and previous teaching experience led to the identification of subject matter experts. Leadership focused on the special traits and strengths of each officer within the agency, and thus determined who would best train FTOs. However, once this process of identification occurred and the trainers were identified, administration delegated full authority to the trainers to develop the training model.

KDPS administration identified me as one they felt embodied the role of internal trainer and asked if I would be interested in conducting a training program for new FTOs internally. I was chosen based on my level of experience as a subject matter expert on field training within the department and my out-of-department teaching abilities. I had been one of the original FTOs since 1993 when the department started the field training program. Also, I had worked in patrol my entire career while serving in multiple specialty units within the patrol division, including the department's SWAT team, Community Policing Unit, and Honor Guard. Having worked all precincts throughout the city of Kalamazoo, my knowledge of the community demographics proved useful in effectively training new FTOs. I also worked at the Kalamazoo Valley Community College Police Academy instructing physical training and subject control, while also serving as an academy drill sergeant mentoring and coaching academy recruits in the development stage of forming civilians into future police officers. I was also a US Army drill sergeant and combat veteran. My military experience and training blended with the criminal justice discipline through my service as a combat advisor in Afghanistan where I mentored, trained, and deployed with the Afghan National Army.

When identifying internal trainers, agencies should capitalize on the knowledge base of their own employees rather than depend on outside-agency instructors when determining who is qualified as an internal subject matter expert.

I was given the timeline for the administration's course implementation and suggested course time period. In an effort to keep overtime costs at a minimum, the administration provided for the training to be conducted in an eight-hour block of instruction. Comparatively, an out-of-agency course was typically one week in duration that would include overtime costs to backfill officers attending training, course fees, food, lodging expenses, and fuel costs.

TRAINING THE FIELD TRAINING OFFICER: NUTS AND BOLTS OF THE TRAINING MODEL

In developing the course, a backward planning concept was used to meet the time requirement, starting with the course date and given an eight-hour day to deliver an effective course that would train over forty new FTOs. With only a month to prepare the new course, a thorough evaluation of the current FTO training process at KDPS was completed. This included concepts from the San Jose, California, police department model and the Glenn Kaminsky Field Training concepts model. Both training concepts had previously been taught to KDPS FTOs. Using these two models, a more specific field training program was developed that was tailored to meet the needs of one of the largest public safety agencies in the United States. Course development included a modern video series, teaching methods, and the miniseries *Rookies* from the Arts & Entertainment Network. The miniseries presented real-life examples of FTOs in action with probationary officers. The show served to be the most effective training tool in demonstrating how an FTO handles the issues of a probationary officer in real-life situations.

While developing the Kalamazoo FTO program, research of other field training models from the Department of Justice was evaluated, and it was discovered that there is no set standard for field training at a national level. In fact, agencies are encouraged by the Department of Justice to formulate their own field training programs that would be agency specific. This allows department trainers to tailor any program to fit their specific department needs.

Many agencies had placed their FTO training models online. The core curricula were almost identical, but many appeared out of touch with what KDPS felt was needed to prepare field training officers to train the modern-day rookie officer.

"As I began to develop our training plan in light of these shortcomings, I began to rely more heavily on my past experiences as a field training officer for eighteen years. The current rookie officer is educated, each having unique career expectations and goals, value systems, and work ethics, and are more inquisitive and quick to question the actions of veteran officers."

The focus was aimed at the adult learner, with a respect for individual differences, and toward improving communication and rapport building between our field training officers and the probationary officers. The end result was an enhanced training experience for the new officers and an increased sense of department pride, stronger work ethic, and more respect toward the veteran officer.

THE KALAMAZOO DIFFERENCE
The Kalamazoo Public Safety FTO program blended the best practices from both the San Jose model and Kaminsky Field Training programs.

Both had been in place since 1993 and were modified to meet the unique challenges that faced a public safety organization while also considering what best practices could be used to enhance the training experience to better prepare the probationary officer for patrol duty.

The Kalamazoo Field Training Program consists of a series of steps targeting administrative goals for the trainers. Field training officers are tasked with helping trainees attain these goals by using phased training methods. The FTO program is a three-month process that covers three shift changes and forty-two work days. Trainees change FTOs three times, switch to three different shifts, work both day and night patrol, and change precincts three times to gain exposure to the diversity of the population of Kalamazoo and to gain experience from three different field training officers.

In creating a new model for how the field training officers could be trained more effectively to help the trainees reach these goals, consideration was given to outcome-based training when developing our new plan. This method would create a more outcome-based field training mind-set in the department and free up field trainers to try different techniques and methods to assist the trainees in attaining departmental goals. In effect, our field training officers could be more creative and goal-oriented, as opposed to being fixed on any one method. Field trainers would be empowered to develop their own training processes through greater freedom and control, meeting the goals of the agency while adjusting methods to suit the trainee's learning needs, and striving to attain the chief's goals and objectives.

When constructing the training program that would provide field trainers with the skills needed to enhance this level of freedom and control, the following topics were incorporated into an eight-hour, classroom-based training segment.

- Commanders intent: a message from the chief
- Mission of the field training unit
- Liability concerns: presented by the FTO commander
- An overview from *The Field Training Concept in Criminal Justice Agencies*, written by Glenn F. Kaminsky (Published by Jeff Johnston, December 23, 2000)
- Department specific training methods and concepts
- FTO duties/responsibilities
- Scenario-based documentation training: *Rookies* miniseries
- End of seminar test of knowledge
- Course evaluation and critique

The training topics were taught in segments embedded in an eight-hour, classroom-based training session. Each segment was no longer than one hour and consisted of lecture, PowerPoint, and video segments to provide situational and scenario-based training and discussion. Breaks were given between each segment followed by a quiz after each break concluded. Class participation and involvement was the key to learning for the group rather than a coffee cup refill and more lecture by a speaker, which is most common during in-service training seminars. The new FTOs were engaged in the tell-show-do method of instruction throughout the segments. In this manner, I showed them how their learning ability was increased and encouraged them to do the same when training their new officers.

The reaction from the FTOs attending the course, including the command staff, was that the in-house training was more effective and tailored to the specific needs of the department when compared to an out-of-agency seminar that was generic in nature.

Financial hardships for police departments don't have to mean they sacrifice the force and ultimately their service delivery to the communities they have sworn to protect and serve. By seeking out alternatives to training and coming up with creative cost-saving ideas, any agency can maintain quality training programs, keep morale high among the ranks, and invest in the quality of its employees. Since this program was initiated in 2011, Kalamazoo Public Safety continues to make improvements to the program and has continued to train and mentor new field training officers for the organization through quality in-house training.

POLICE ACADEMY TRAINING

We Build Police Officers

I began my teaching profession in 1997 at Kalamazoo Valley Community College. I owe the beginning of my professional teaching career to Jeff Shouldice. Jeff originally hired me to teach part-time for him as part of the two-year criminal justice associate's degree program. The course was "Patrol Techniques." Over the next three years, the criminal justice program at KVCC was modified to also include the regional police academy where my focus was then shifted to my area of expertise: physical training and subject control. I was teamed up with Paul Bianco, a fellow Kalamazoo public safety officer and also a US Army drill sergeant. What a great combination! Two former army drill sergeants tasked with mentoring, coaching, and transitioning civilians into police officers. I could not have asked for a better part-time job. Jeff was instrumental in not only combining the two programs at the college, but also in setting a platform for the program to excel and grow throughout the next several years.

As Paul Bianco and I took on our new mission of training police academy recruits, we found that not only were we keeping ourselves in great physical shape by instructing and leading every physical training session, but we also found that teaching in the academy kept our tactical skills sharp. We still performed our duties as Kalamazoo public safety officers, and teaching gave us a tactical edge during our patrol functions. In addition, teaching enhanced our credibility as subject matter experts in the eyes of the police recruits who were counting on us to give them the best possible basic training experience they could receive.

As the years continued and the many academies came and went, we saw our new officers go on to become the future of law enforcement. I felt as though I had come a long way in my career from March 4, 1990 and the physical altercation I had with Juan Rico where I nearly lost my life due in part to a lack of proper training and mental preparation for a life-and-death situation. Now I was tasked to help guarantee my students would not meet this same fate, or at least help them be more prepared to handle a physical altercation so that they could live to fight another day.

In my travels around the country and to other police academies, I have seen many different training techniques, but at Kalamazoo Valley Community College there is one thing that I have yet to see at any another academy. At KVCC every drill instructor is a US Army trained and certified drill sergeant who has had the experiences of building soldiers in a military environment while also working as a police officer.

In many academies, you have what are called drill instructors. These instructors are tasked with performing the transition process that makes a civilian into a self-motivated, proactive police officer who possesses a positive work ethic and embodies the attributes that make up the law enforcement professional. They create a new police officer who exemplifies professionalism by holding true to the Constitution of the United States.

At the KVCC Academy, to hold the title of drill sergeant, you *must* really be a drill sergeant. It is not simply a title. It is a time-honored position and one that is earned.

I am a Drill Sergeant

I will assist each individual in their efforts to become a highly motivated,
Well-disciplined, physically and mentally fit soldier,
capable of defeating any enemy on today's modern battlefield.
I will instill pride in all I train. Pride in self, in the army, and in country.
I will insist that each soldier meets and maintains the army standards of military bearing and courtesy, consistent with the highest traditions of the US Army.
I will lead by example, never requiring a soldier
to attempt any task I would not do myself.
But first, last, and always, I am an American soldier sworn to defend
the Constitution of the United States against all enemies, both foreign and
domestic.

I am a Drill Sergeant.

(Information on the history of the US Army Drill Sergeant and Drill Sergeant training can be found at http://www.jackson.army.mil/sites/dss/docs/1068)

Sometimes, we see the very best in our academy recruits and in one rare instance we see a future drill sergeant. Keaton Nielsen attended our academy upon returning from an Iraq deployment with the US Army and was attending Western Michigan University to pursue his dream of becoming a police officer. While Drill Sergeant Bianco and I were mentoring him in the academy, we noticed that Cadet Nielsen possessed those rare traits that we see in future drill sergeants. At the time, Cadet Nielsen was still a member of the army reserves. I was in between reenlistments with my own military service obligation and was actually contemplating hanging up my military career and simply continuing to serve the community through my law enforcement career. However, something magical happened to me, and I owe it all to Keaton Nielsen and Paul Bianco.

In January of 2006, Cadet Nielsen was attending the police academy. One day at the end of our subject control training, Paul and I called Nielsen into our drill sergeant office. We both told him how we thought that he possessed the special leadership traits needed to one day become a US Army drill sergeant. I could see in Nielsen's face that he was surprised and excited to see that his drill sergeants were complimenting him on his leadership potential. However, there was just one thing I felt he needed to push him over the contemplation phase of considering becoming a drill sergeant and to actually do it. I too was on the fence, and looking back I realized that it was really *me* that needed to be pushed out of my comfort zone.

I challenged young Nielsen: "Listen! You transfer into the drill sergeant unit in Kalamazoo and agree to attend drill sergeant school, and I'll reenlist in the army and join your same unit."

My hand reached out to him. Without any hesitation Nielsen took my hand and said, "Deal." The bet was sealed and the challenge was given.

"Now get out of here," barked Drill Sergeant Bianco. Paul turned to me, "You realize what you just did, right?" He laughed, but then he stopped and gave me his serious look.

"I do. I think I just joined the army again," I said.

This would be the best bet I ever lost. It was only a few weeks later that Cadet Nielsen showed me proof that he had completed his transfer in the army reserves and joined the 2/330th Infantry Regiment in Kalamazoo, Michigan. I followed through with my end of the deal and reenlisted myself into the US Army Reserve under an indefinite contract on February 22, 2007.

Shortly after Keaton graduated from the police academy and Western Michigan University, he was hired by Kalamazoo Public Safety and attended the US Army Drill Sergeant School. As the years progressed, Keaton was also hired onto our training staff within the police academy where all three of us then teamed up to train and mentor the aspiring new police officers entrusted to our care. We make a great team.

The years to follow would be some of the best times of my military career. I went on to volunteer for a year-long mobilization to Fort Benning, Georgia, assigned to both the 1/330th Infantry and 2/58th Infantry where I served as a senior drill sergeant training/mentoring and sending hundreds of US infantrymen to both Iraq and Afghanistan.

In 2009 I volunteered and deployed to Afghanistan as a combat advisor. I helped to establish basic training for the Afghanistan National Army and helped to mentor my Afghan counterparts on how to impart infantry tactics to a new breed of Afghanistan soldiers. In another ironic twist of events, in 2009 Drill Sergeant Nielsen also volunteered for this same Afghanistan mission, and we deployed together. In Keaton's words: "I can't let you go to war without me." I am forever grateful for the friendship that I have with both Keaton Nielsen and Paul Bianco. They are truly my warrior brothers.

Why do we do it? All three of us have great jobs working full-time as police officers, so why would we need another part-time job? Believe it or not, we don't do it for the money. Sure, the part-time supplemental income is nice, but we see our obligation to train and mentor our new officers as a moral obligation that we have, and one that we owe to our chosen profession. If we chose not to do it, we would be doing a disservice to our fellow professionals. Admittedly, working a twelve-hour shift all night long yet showing up to teach at the academy for three hours certainly took its toll on our bodies. There were days that I just wanted to drive home and go to sleep, but I could never do it. I knew I had an academy class waiting for me, counting on us to be there for them. We showed the trainees through our own example that we cared so much for them and their training that we would sacrifice our own personal time to commit ourselves 100 percent to them, without regard for our own comfort level. This, I feel is the mark of a true leader.

Here is some advice for those who dream about becoming a police officer. The following is what you can do to help prepare yourself for success when you attend a police academy. You must be fully committed to your basic training academy and adjust your life accordingly, both personally and financially, so that you can focus all of your attention on the training you are about to embark upon. Don't think that you can put forth anything less than 100 percent of your effort into your training. The training you receive at the academy will set the stage for your entire career.

FOLLOW THESE SUGGESTIONS BY PAST ACADEMY CADETS:

- Study more intensely in the beginning of the academy.
- Be more "academic focused."
- Be more vocal and outspoken when in a leadership role.

- Be totally committed during the academy and explain this to your family.
- Be more prepared physically, especially with cardiovascular.
- Be prepared for the obstacles presented by the physical training.
- Understand that "college was effortless" compared to the academy.
- Spread the studying out instead of cramming.
- Come out of your shell and step up more often.
- Be in bed no later than 2200 hours to be rested.
- Be more social and involved with the other cadets.
- Consider military service before coming to the academy.
- Seek out employment in the early weeks and research departments while in the academy.
- Stay fresh mentally and physically; start reading to get your mind ready.
- Know that you might need to lose weight before starting the academy. One cadet stated, "I dropped thirty-five pounds before coming here."

They shall be my finest warriors, these people who give themselves to me.
Like clay I shall mold them and in the furnace of war I shall forge them.
They will be of iron will and steely muscle.
In armor I shall clad them and with the mightiest guns shall they be armed.
They will have tactics, strategies, and machines such that
no foe shall best them in battle.
They are my bulwark against the terror.

They are defenders of freedom.
They are the police and they shall know no fear.
Original poem by Mark English, Drill Sergeant US Army who I was hon-
ored to serve with at Ft. Benning, Georgia in 2007. Edited by Robert T.
Christensen to be applicable for police officers.

COMMUNITY POLICING

I'm not going to repeat what's been said so many times about community policing theories. What I will tell you is what worked and what didn't work while I was a community police officer in Kalamazoo's Edison neighborhood.

First, I must say that the five years I was a neighborhood liaison officer, now referred to as a community police officer (CPO), were the five most rewarding years of my career. The relationships and bonds of trust that I developed during this time continue still to this day even after my retirement. I will be forever grateful for the hard work and dedication of the neighborhood workers I had the privilege to serve with and the community members and business leaders who helped foster a crime reduction effort to improve the quality of life for our residents.

When the police, citizens, local government, politicians, community action groups, businesses, local media, schools, faith-based organizations, and the street patrol officers work together, amazing things can happen. Collaboration is the key to success.

Essentially, as a CPO, my duties were to be an ambassador of the city of Kalamazoo for my assigned neighborhood. With that, I was given the flexibility to create my own projects and initiatives, all aimed at improving the quality of life for the residents I served through crime reduction efforts. In addition, I was tasked with fostering and building a stronger relationship between every aspect of the community, police, and local government. This means I was truly an ambassador of the city and for the city. I was the direct link, and on many occasions, the *voice* of the people I swore to serve and protect and the link between them and the chief of police, mayor, city commissioners, prosecuting attorney, city attorney, and local media. I was doing the same job as a CPO that I would find myself doing as a combat advisor in Afghanistan in 2009–2010. I am confident that it was the experience I gained in Kalamazoo that led to my success as an army advisor when I deployed to Afghanistan. The two jobs were very similar.

I hope that all police officers find themselves in a position to be a community police officer. In fact, every single one of you really is a community police officer, if you are doing your job properly. I'm going to tell you how my daily routine was managed, and it is my hope that you can understand the massive amount of responsibility you have and the great things you can do to change a community, if you do your job properly.

First of all, let's talk about building relationships. This is the key to your success. This job cannot be done behind the wheel of a patrol car. It requires a personal touch that you have to force yourself to do in order to foster the relationships necessary for success. Remember, you're trying to be creative and reduce crime. So, it's time to stop being a patrol officer and adjust your tactics accordingly.

When I started out as a CPO I already had a plan in my mind. I wanted to be assigned the highest crime-rate neighborhood with the most diverse population our city had to offer. That was the Edison neighborhood—the largest by size and population of all city neighborhoods. With that, comes a higher crime rate. Not to mention, this neighborhood was one that saw high unemployment and a high poverty rate, with mostly rental properties and a low number of home ownerships. I'll come back to the attributes of the neighborhood later when I discuss the federal weed-and-seed initiative. My goal was to make a difference. I needed some quick wins!

Kalamazoo Public Safety had a solid and established community policing unit already in place throughout the city with representation in all city neighborhoods. Edison had two assigned CPOs: my partner, Craig Johnson, and me. Our call signs were Baker Twenty-eight and Baker Twenty-nine. Our offices were located in the neighborhood and not in the police station. We were located inside the United Methodist Church in the heart of the neighborhood alongside the Edison Neighborhood Association. With that we were fortunate to have our own neighborhood prosecuting attorneys, Karen Hayter and Rami Almeda. Talk about a team effort! The police, the prosecutor's office, and the neighborhood association teamed up and communicated on a daily basis as we were all focused on improving the quality of life for the neighborhood. During my time as a CPO, Officer Craig Johnson completed his service time, and I was honored to have a new partner in crime, Officer Tim Randall. Tim was like a Tasmanian devil; he was so full of energy and ideas. He took the reins and continued to serve honorably in his position after I had been transferred back to the patrol division after five years of CPO duty.

When I started my new position I began the relationship-building process. I purchased a cell phone and kept it on me at all times. I wanted the neighborhood association to have direct communication with me and to not have to call KDPS dispatch to find or speak to a police officer. Yes, I belonged to the neighborhood and any problem, even if it wasn't a police matter, was my problem also. On duty or off duty, I didn't care. I was always a phone call away.

Our offices surely didn't amount to anything—a small desk, city telephone, and file cabinets. Our telephones were another link to the citizens. Often I would receive citizen complaints of an ongoing nature with which I would start out my day. These calls would commonly include over twenty voice mail messages from crimes such as barking dogs and drug dealing, to tips on homicides or prostitution complaints. I would make sure that every phone call was returned, or I would go to the address and make personal contact with the citizen who called me for assistance. Remember, my job was to *solve* the ongoing complaint, not simply to respond and disposition the call then go to the next, which is what patrol typically does. I had time on my side. Since I wasn't burdened with the constant calls for service that the street officers were dealing with, I would take the time needed to investigate, refer, or conduct undercover operations in an attempt to resolve the situation through mediation, enforcement, or prosecution. Remember, we are doing surgery, not just applying bandages to fix a problem.

The majority of my voicemails were noise violations, drug dealings, prostitution complaints, trespassing issues, or junked and abandoned vehicles. Many times I would simply have to educate the public that if there was a crime in progress to immediately call the patrol police and to then call me. Otherwise, I would never know a problem existed. I guess this was the frustrating part for me. There was a lack of communication between the patrol division and the community policing unit. I had to take the initiative and get the daily calls for service, review them, and choose which ones I felt were ongoing in nature that I could resolve. Remember, too, I was still a *real cop* and fostering a relationship with the patrol officers of the zone while still taking care of the needs of the community.

So, making personal contact with the players of the community was at the top of my list. That included the neighborhood association, business associations, zoning enforcement officers, housing inspectors, and neighborhood block watch members (commonly called *neighborhood watch*). Attending meetings was a daily episode, but it has to be done. By attending every type of community meeting in the neighborhood, you instantly set a feeling of partnership between the police and community. Oftentimes at these meetings, I would be asked questions or given an opportunity to speak on behalf of the department. Never pass up an opportunity to speak at these meetings. Your goal is to build relationships and establish lines of communication. The community must feel that you are genuinely concerned for their wellbeing if you are to have their support in crime reduction efforts. Keep in mind the idea of the *team effort* as you go on.

Next I wanted a quick win, one that would make a visible difference and spawn interest in the community by its citizens to become more involved. I developed my own initiative called the Grow Team Initiative. The Grow Team Initiative was an effort to eliminate all junk autos, blight, and trash complaints from the neighborhood. The Edison neighborhood was clearly a dumping ground and looked like crap. We are not just talking a few junk cars either. In the course of three years, I had personally removed over fifteen hundred junk vehicles from private property locations and streamlined the referral process for junk, litter, housing, and zoning violations, not only in the Edison neighborhood, but also throughout the city. To bring attention to the problem, I contacted the local television, radio, and newspaper to create a story about the epidemic and the efforts the police department and neighborhood association were making to address the problem.

My goal to include the media was twofold. The first part was to bring attention to the issue and to show the community that the department was taking action. I wanted to also inspire and motivate individual property owners and landlords to see that enforcement was being done and to help encourage them to clean up their own property before prosecution was initiated against them. The second part was to include the media as a partner, not an adversary, in working to bring the matter to the attention of the city and to show that the department (which is the city, too) was in fact doing proactive measures to reduce the accumulation of junk, rubbish, and junk cars.

Was this a first? Absolutely not. I was following the broken-windows theory of community policing introduced by James Wilson and George Kelling during the mid-1970s. Accessed from: http://www.theatlantic.com/magazine/archive/1982/03/broken-windows/304465/ on March 1, 2014 at 4:00 p.m. The plan was to improve the neighborhood and make it undesirable for criminal behavior. A neighborhood that looks like it is not cared for because of poor design, poor lighting, street-level drug dealing, prostitution, loitering, roaming bands of youth, (especially those that walk in the middle of the street), curfew violations, and other public-order crimes that are visible simply attract more of the criminal element. The Grow Team Initiative was the first of many other initiatives that would eventually lead to the reduction of crime in the Edison neighborhood. This stuff really works!

Certainly, I was only a piece of the machine that was already working to reduce crime and grow the community. My part as a community police officer was just one aspect of the program that went along with the efforts of many other service groups working to improve the area. At the same time I became a CPO, there was a planning group already in place called the Edison Weed and Seed steering committee. This group was creating a design and application process in an effort to secure federal funding for the Edison neighborhood to be designated as a federal Weed and Seed Neighborhood Revitalization site. The partners involved with the steering committee were Kalamazoo Public Safety, City of Kalamazoo, Edison Neighborhood Association, Edison Business Association, Kalamazoo County Prosecutors Office, US Attorney's Office, Edison Main Street Program, Partners Building Community, Local Initiatives Support Corporation, and local residents. The program was a collaborated effort by all parties involved to meet the seven goals as set out by the committee over a five-year period from 2000 to 2005.

The City of Kalamazoo's Edison neighborhood was established as a federal weed and seed neighborhood by the US Department of Justice Community Capacity Development Office in 2000 and received funding for a five-year program to coordinate the following activities:

1. Reduce Part 1 crime by 5 percent.
2. Eliminate abandoned cars and accumulation of trash.
3. Reduce youth crime by 10 percent.
4. Reduce curfew violations in the neighborhood by a visible amount.
5. Improve attendance at public schools by Edison youth by 10 percent.
6. Create a family oriented retail shopping district.
7. Improve the appearance and safety of homes in the neighborhood.

The overall program was deemed a success and resulted in essentially a neighborhood overhaul and revitalization of the Edison neighborhood. The goals outlined were not only met but exceeded through continued partnerships and a grassroots effort to involve the residents of the neighborhood in taking ownership of the Edison neighborhood.

In addition to the committee goals, other major developments included the reduction of recidivism and the development of Operation NEAT. The team met with returning parolees and probationers from prison and jail eight times per year to assist them in their transition back to the civilian community and to help ensure compliance with the terms of their release. Kalamazoo Public Safety and the city housing department acquired property and built a community policing mini-station within the neighborhood that was accessible to local residents. Crime Prevention through Environmental Design (CPTED) techniques were also incorporated, and an additional 2.3 million dollars were provided to support local businesses in a corridor area to help revitalize storefronts and to help ensure long-term crime prevention techniques.

All graffiti throughout the neighborhood was removed, abandoned homes were updated or razed, and over two thousand junk automobiles were removed. The sexually oriented adult businesses along the main corridor were relocated, and prostitution came to a halt. Most significant over the five-year period was the reduction in part-one crime by 24 percent. The five-year period also saw federally funded overtime to implement curfew sweeps by police. We also initiated an aggressive response to illegal drug activity in the neighborhood, addressed quality-of-life crimes (just as in the Newark, New Jersey, foot patrol experiment), improved police-citizen relationships, and made a focused effort to eradicate street level drug dealing, assaults, juvenile crime, and prostitution.

The federal Weed and Seed Program was developed to assist law enforcement and community revitalization efforts while attempting to control violent crime, drug abuse, and gang activity. The federal involvement with local communities can be seen as a last ditch effort to save the affected community. Essentially, the program is meant to weed out crime and seed the resources for neighborhood revitalization. In 2000 the program was implemented in one hundred and fifty communities across the country and funded through the US Department of Justice.

Through all of this hard work to reduce crime and grow the local economy, you would think the Edison neighborhood is a wonderful place now, right? Unfortunately, there is a sad reality to all of my efforts as a CPO. I would agree that the neighborhood clearly made some improvements during this time. However, like anything else, you have to maintain it and continue to take care of the quality-of-life issues or the crime will return. Sadly, that's exactly what happened. From 2010 to 2011, I worked the Edison neighborhood, not as a community policing officer, but as a patrol officer, and I found that since I had left in 2005 the neighborhood had reverted back to how it was when the process to improve began back in 1999. I was very disappointed.

MAKE IMPROVEMENTS AND CONDUCT MAINTENANCE TO SUSTAIN A COMMUNITY

I want to share with you one story that goes to show how a street officer with a sense of work ethic can help to make a difference and take care of a community.

In March of 2012, I was dispatched to an intersection in the Edison neighborhood because of a report of kids at the bus stop smashing windows out of the house located there. Here was an abandoned home in bank foreclosure and completely painted in rival gang graffiti, including the back fence and garage. Every window had been broken out of the home, and the small windows on the front door were smashed. There was a side door open and casual entry could be made. An interior check of the structure found evidence of vagrants taking up residency and signs of drug use with crack cocaine paraphernalia on the floor. There was interior damage to the structure as well. The grass was already growing out of control and a condemned building sign was posted high on the front porch wall by the city.

What upset me most was a mother waiting with her daughter at the bus stop who saw me walking around the house while I took pictures. She said, "Thank God, you're finally doing something about that place. I have called the city and nothing ever gets done!" After our conversation she recognized me from seven years earlier when I worked this same neighborhood as an CPO.

I told her that I would not rest until this house was fixed or torn down.

She said, "Well, Officer Todd, I'll believe it when I see it."

I felt terrible, to say the least, and even more obligated to follow through and fix the problem myself, if need be. I, too, was upset and wondered why the current CPO and related associations had not addressed this issue before it became a patrol problem.

Here is how I fixed the problem: through collaboration and bringing attention to an ongoing neighborhood issue and by dealing diplomatically with the supervisor of the city-housing department, Tim Meulenberg. Tim and I worked closely during the Edison Weed and Seed initiatives from 2000 to 2005, so the relationship that we had built in the past helped me solve this problem.

The home in question had been condemned by the city; therefore, part of the burden fell upon the city's shoulders. The landowner had been given notice previously to clean up the property or the city would seize it, and he would lose the house and land. The case had simply not been followed up on. All it took was a phone call, followed by a contact with a Kalamazoo city commissioner and a county commissioner, to bring the property owner into compliance. Within one week, the house was repaired completely and repainted. The back fence was replaced, and the yard mowed.

I knew I had succeeded, not by the home being repaired, but when I saw the female resident while on patrol and she mouthed a thank-you and gave me a thumbs-up. That was all I needed.

DON'T BE A LAW ENFORCEMENT OFFICER; BE A POLICE OFFICER

Do you want to make a difference as a cop? Then stop being a law enforcement officer and start being a police officer again. For example, in the Hays Park area, a known drug corridor in Kalamazoo, there is a notable difference when a group of just three PSOs are on foot patrol simply walking in public view along city streets and sidewalks. They take the time to stop to talk to residents and children playing in the street. At the same time, they address quality-of-life issues, such as illegal parking, junk automobiles, excessive noise, loud car stereos, loitering on street corners, littering, public drunkenness, fights, and other minor offenses. They also prohibit roving bands of youth from walking in the street. The effect of this visibility is the noticeable reduction in street-level drug dealing.

The street-level drug dealing essentially disappears in less than thirty minutes after the officers come out on foot patrol. In comparison, a mass of police cruisers driving through the area has little to no effect on controlling or reducing street-level drug dealing. I would contribute this behavior to a human instinct that a lawbreaker does not want anything to do with the personal contact of a police officer for fear of apprehension and investigation. The simple passing by of a police car is no threat to these individuals, unless the officer stops and exits the cruiser to begin an investigation. Even then the drug dealers will watch the actions of the officer to determine whether or not the officer is deemed a threat to their personal liberty.

Do you want to make a difference as a cop? Then stop being a law enforcement officer and start being a police officer again. Get out of the car, walk your beat, visit with business owners, shake hands with people, and say hello to them. Develop a rapport and know people by their first names. Get on your bike and ride with kids. Stop to play basketball with them. Break down the barriers that exist between you and the people you swore to protect and serve. There is a time and a place for everything, but you must never forget you work for the people, and you are more than just an enforcer. Be a cop!

FIREFIGHTING AND EMS

"Too often, we underestimate the power of a touch, a smile, a kind word,
a listening ear, an honest compliment, or the smallest act of caring,
all of which have the potential to turn a life around."
Leo Buscaglia

In Kalamazoo, a public safety officer's duties were about 85 percent police-related work. The remainder of our time was spent in the realm of fire and EMS. In Kalamazoo, all officers are cross-trained as police officers, firefighters, and medical first responders. As a PSO conducts patrol, each officer carries a pack containing fire protective gear. In the trunk of a patrol car are a self-contained breathing apparatus (SCBA) and a medical bag that contains the essentials a medical first responder (MFR) would need to provide basic care and an external defibrillator.

While PSOs are on patrol, they are assigned specific zones within the city and, for each zone, is a fire station. Two different radio tones are dispatched for fire or medical calls. Depending on the location and the type of call, a response would typically involve sending the fire apparatus and the assigned PSOs from that zone, or a PSO would also respond to a priority-one medical call along with the KDPS Medical Rescue vehicle from the assigned station for each zone.

One of the advantages to a public safety department, as opposed to a separate police department, is a very quick response to any type of fire or medical emergency. However, there is one big downside to the public safety model. In a fire emergency, there are few if any police officers on patrol. Two structure fires on opposite sides of the city would many times degrade the police presence to zero, because all the street PSOs were working at their respective fire scenes. With that, other agencies are requested to respond to major police incidents, or in many cases the calls simply get stacked until a PSO becomes available then the police calls for service would be handled. The only type of police call that officers were not allowed to leave in order to respond to a fire were a drunk-driving investigation when a chemical test was being administered. Other than that, all officers were expected to stop what they were doing and respond to the fire. This situation created frustration on the part of the citizenry and a breakdown in our customer service delivery.

Firefighting was a total rush for me! The best part of firefighting for me was being first on scene—well before the fire truck would arrive. The first arriving PSO was able to perform a size-up for other respond-ing units. You were able to get suited up in your fire gear and, if needed, a quick search and rescue could be initiated without having to wait for a fire truck to arrive. I found that many times I was able to be dressed and "on air" waiting for the engine to arrive. You can't get any faster than that! I found that I loved being on the nozzle of the first line in the door. Doing battle with "the dragon," as we called it, was clearly a full-on rush of adrenaline.

My only serious injury as a public safety officer, though, took place while firefighting. Unlike in Lawrence where I got my ass kicked by Juan Rico, I was fortunate enough to suffer only minor scuffs and scrapes while fighting with other suspects. Fire, on the other hand, was unmerciful, unpredictable, and very dangerous.

"Report of a structure fire, 3700 Emerald Drive. Apparatus to respond Engine Two, Engine Seven, Engine Six, and Truck Six."

This call came out right around seven thirty in the evening. It was just after shift change, and I had been assigned to work on Truck Six rather than street duty. What's really screwed up is that I remember seeing the plume of black smoke coming up from the east side of the city as I pulled into work, but the fire had not been noticed yet. Many times, a PSO would be assigned what we called "rig duty" when street staffing levels were over strength and station personnel levels were under strength. Typically, this would mean that a street PSO would have an enjoyable night of a few medical calls to respond to or maybe a fire, but usually it would result in a relaxing night of catching up on follow-up reports, getting in a workout, and having a solid eight hours of sleep. That was certainly not the case during this structure fire. A large commercial building was on fire, and it would take two days to extinguish the flames. I would find myself nearly killed within an hour of starting my shift.

I responded on Truck Six to the scene. Once on scene there was a sense of panic and a feeling of urgency. The building was a working structure fire with flames coming out of the roof. With the adrenaline flowing, I found myself entering a terrible and possibly life-threatening situation. I had walked out onto the end of the ladder while it was still on the truck in an effort to attach the nozzle. As I was on the ladder, it began to rise up and extend out over the roof on fire. I really don't think the engine operator knew that I was on the ladder and was simply putting the ladder in position. I put myself in this dangerous position. As the ladder was extending outward, my right boot became trapped in the rungs, and I could feel my foot and leg being pulled down into the ladder. I tried to pull my foot out of my boot, and thank God I did, because the ladder was unforgiving and would have snapped my leg in half. Instead, it pulled the boot completely off my foot. So there I was struggling to attach the nozzle onto the end of the moving ladder, with one boot and one sock on my feet.

Once the ladder was moved away from the truck, it was being extended out toward the fire. With a large bang, the ladder fell downward into the power lines. I felt myself up in the air, hovering and then slamming chest first back down on the ladder, sparks flying everywhere. I was then just below the top of the power pole off the ground, and I remember still looking down at the ground, lying on my chest.

The shift lieutenant on the ground below me looked up and yelled, "God dammit, Todd, get the hell off that thing!" I was in complete agreement and slowly made my way away from the heat of the flames and crawled my way back down the ladder. The ladder had failed to support itself because it had been extended out away from the truck at too low a level.

Once I got off the ladder, the lieutenant grabbed me, put his hand on top of my helmet, pointed me in the direction of a nearby ambulance, and told me to go get checked out. The lieutenant must have seen something that I was oblivious to, because he wasted no time in getting me into that ambulance.

The only pain I had was in my right foot that had been pinned in the ladder rungs. The ambulance transported me to Bronson Hospital, and when I was in the ER I explained to the doc that I was on the ladder, had my leg and foot pinned in the ladder rungs, and was dropped into power lines. I was very lucky that I wasn't electrocuted and killed instantly.

When I was in the emergency room, Deputy Chief Grigsby stopped by to check on me. I felt great about this, even as a young officer, that one of the department's chiefs would come and check on me in the hospital. I gained a lot of respect for our administration and continued to have the highest level of faith and trust in the leaders of my department throughout my career. About eleven o'clock that same night, I was released from the hospital and allowed to go home and take sick time for the rest of my shift. I was forever skeptical of the ladder trucks from that day forward and tried to avoid them if at all possible during fires.

Firefighting in general in Kalamazoo was a total rush. I was most impressed with our ability to effectively use the incident command system. Everyone knew exactly what was supposed to happen at a scene. Fires were so frequent that they actual became routine for us. Our scenes were not without total chaos though. Like any evolving fire scene, emotions run high. I will say, though, that at the end of day the fire was out and our officers saved many lives, including our own at times.

The emergency medical services side of the house was more passionate for me. As an army combat medic since I was seventeen and starting out in Lawrence as a medical first responder and then obtaining my emergency medical technician license, I found that the EMS services were my base. I thoroughly enjoyed saving lives and dealing with people on more of a personal level. In Kalamazoo I was exposed to a multitude of memorable medical calls that I felt worthy of remembering and sharing with others.

"Baker Eleven and Twelve, respond with Engine Seven to Lowden Street for a subject stabbed in the chest with a knife."

Right out of briefing at Station Six to a stabbing call. Awesome! Way to start the shift. Welcome to Kalamazoo. I would have never imagined that by eight thirty in the evening, less than two hours into my shift, I'd be holding onto a human heart. God, I loved my job!

We arrived on scene to find a male subject who had been stabbed in the chest with a large kitchen knife. His roommate had stabbed him as a result of an altercation and was taken into custody by my partner. I went to the aid of the victim and assisted paramedics. The victim was still breathing but in severe respiratory distress and crashing fast. His heart rate was increasing, and breathing was becoming more difficult. This was a load-and-go situation, and the paramedics wasted no time getting the victim into the ambulance and rushing to Bronson Hospital. I rode in the ambulance. On this particular day, William Fales, MD, who was also the Kalamazoo County Medical Control Director, had arrived on scene and was also in the back of the ambulance. Doc Fales was an EMS guru and loved emergency medicine. While in the back of the ambulance, I started to give rescue breaths to assist the victim, as his breathing became worse. He was suffering from a pneumothorax. The knife was moving with every beat of the heart, as it was secured in place with bandages around his chest. Unfortunately though, the knife had also punctured his lung, causing the breathing difficulty. Doc Fales performed a maneuver to relieve the tension of the pneumothorax by inserting a large bore needle between the victim's ribs to relieve the buildup of air pressure in his chest cavity in an effort to help him breath. Bright red blood was starting to leak through the pile of bandages around the knife and the victim was unconscious and not breathing on his own.

We wheeled into the emergency department, and the victim was rushed to the trauma room. He went into cardiac arrest, and emergency surgery was performed right before my eyes. I was still assisting with breathing by pushing air into his lungs with a bag valve mask. The heart was exposed as the surgeons worked to plug up the holes and lacerations left by the knife once it was removed. The heart was quivering and shaking. Electrodes were applied directly to the heart, and it was shocked over and over in an effort to bring it back to a normal heartbeat. For all of our rescue efforts, this man died as a result of the stab wounds.

When the chaos of the situation had passed, and the victim was pronounced dead in the emergency room, the scene turned into a massive training episode for the ER staff and new intern/resident medical doctors assigned to the hospital. I remember that Dr. Fales made it a point to show each physician how the heart and lungs were injured from the stabbing.

I was standing out of the way and washing my hands when Doc Fales called out to me, "Hey, Todd, you want to feel this guy's heart?"

"Well, sure." I gloved back up and Doc Fales told me to just reach inside the victim's chest and feel the heart. I was amazed at how big the human heart was and how hard it actually felt in my hand. Never in my mind would I have imagined that in less than two hours of starting my shift that I would be holding onto another man's heart. This was truly an amazing moment. Yeah, it really sucked that this guy died, but when you take a knife to the heart, that's probably what's going to happen. I was more impressed with the efforts we did as a team to try to save his life and with the after-the-fact biology training session that it turned into. Dr. Fales is a true professional in every way.

This wasn't the first time Dr. Fales and I had worked together. In 1995, Dr. Fales and Bobby Hopewell, the manager of the Kalamazoo station of the LIFE EMS Ambulance Service, worked to put together the Kalamazoo Public Safety SWAT Medic program. This was a program to include LIFE Paramedics during SWAT call-ups so that advanced life support measures were present during all SWAT-related events. The purpose was to increase the likelihood that life-saving measures would be available for both officers and suspects during high-risk situations. It was always an honor to work with both Dr. Fales and Bobby Hopewell. Bobby Hopewell and I would grow to become good friends in the years to come. After his employment with LIFE EMS, Bobby would go on to become a Kalamazoo city commissioner and then mayor of Kalamazoo. He continues to serve as mayor as of this writing.

"Radio Baker Eleven, respond to 700 Academy Street
for the neighbors calling to report a foul odor."

It was August of 1993, and the dog days of summer were heating up. It was a typical early evening night in Michigan with the heat of the day still lingering and 100 percent humidity. It was the type of summer day when the air conditioning runs constantly, and one where you made sure you carried water in the cruiser and had the air on but still kept your windows cracked. The only way to cool down your body was to get the cruiser up to at least thirty-five miles per hour, stick your left arm out the window to get the wind blowing inside the sleeve of your shirt, and pull your vest out away from your chest to get airflow between the bulletproof vest and your skin. Yeah, now you know how hot it was.

I walked around the outside of the large three-story house that had been turned into a duplex. I made my way around the east side of the house and was hit in the face by the pungent odor of rotting human flesh. I looked around and found an open basement window only partially seen through the tall grass on the property. The window was covered with flies, and the smell was putrid. On my hands and knees, I peered inside the window to see a body lying on the bathroom floor and wedged between the toilet and the wall. This person, whoever he was, would soon become known as Maggot Man.

I followed our general order for handling a dead body. I notified the landlord notification and my supervisor, and requested an ambulance and the funeral home body recovery team. Of course, there was no rush. It's not like we were going to save his life. The door to the apartment was locked, so I entered the apartment by opening up the basement window and removing the screen. I had to take off my uniform shirt, vest, and gun belt to fit my body through the tight space of the basement window and then inch my way down onto the floor. The smell was overpowering! Once inside the apartment, which was a good ninety degrees or more, I found an infestation of large green flies, the type of fly that only death attracts. I made my way through the apartment, holding my breath, and found the front door to make my escape. By this time my zone partner had arrived, along with the street supervisor and paramedics with an ambulance.

The scene was secured. It was later determined that the death wasn't suspicious in nature but one of natural causes. The decaying man had been dead for about three days according to detectives, based on the condition of the body. Crime lab technicians deemed the scene to not be a crime scene, so it was time to remove the body.

I was then strapped into my self-contained breathing apparatus (SCBA) that was normally used during fire suppression activity, but the stench was just intolerable. Even the ambulance paramedics were in SCBA. The lab technician who came to the scene rubbed Vicks VapoRub® under his nose to help control the disgusting smell.

A closer examination of the body revealed an even more disturbing sight. The eyes, ears, and nose of the man were all decayed, exposing the inside of his head and brain area. The area of his head was crawling with maggots and flies. It was the most disturbing sight I had seen in my career thus far. His skin was blackened and the body bloated to the point where the buttons on his shirt looked like they were ready to pop. As we pulled and tugged on the man to free him from the area where he was wedged between the toilet and the wall, I had hold of his right arm. In the process of pulling him away from the wall, a large section of his arm peeled off the bone. I lost my balance and fell backward onto the floor, still holding onto this bloated, bloody, fluid-oozing arm of a man. I was screaming in my facemask!

I yelled, "Oh God!" But at the same time, I was laughing at my coworkers, who were also helping to free Maggot Man from his predicament. One paramedic threw up in his mask and took off running for the apartment door. Disgusting pieces of Maggot Man were dripping all over the place, covering our biohazard suits with yellow juice, rotted blood, maggots, and goop.

So, how do cops and EMS personnel handle such disgusting calls? We laugh, joke, and laugh some more, once it's all said and done. Taking a shower helps too. The debauchery of jokes and jabs to one another goes on for years afterward. I think I would have gone completely mad from my career had it not been for all of the laughs and humor we had at work. I mean, come on. How many times would this happen to a "normal person?" I don't even know what normal is anymore.

DIVINE INTERVENTION?

One day before my second suspension was to be in effect (the big fifteen-day suspension for the comp time debacle), I was still working as an Edison community policing officer and was on patrol in the downtown area simply driving around and thinking about my career and life with a fresh mocha.

It was a cool December night, and I was waiting for my shift to come to an end. I had just been notified that I was facing a month off work, reduction in pay, and transfer back to patrol. I was totally depressed and hating myself.

The rescue tones went out for a woman in labor on the third floor of the Radisson Plaza Hotel. It was as if the tones woke me back up and brought me back to reality. Well, shit, I'm right here! I was just driving past the back loading dock of the hotel when the call came out. At the same time, I was being flagged down by hotel staff waving their arms in the air at the back dock of the hotel.

"Radio Baker Twenty-eight, show me out at the Radisson. Reference the Rescue call."

I donned my medical gloves and walked into the back door of the hotel.

The staff person who greeted me was in a state of panic. "She's upstairs in the laundry room," she said.

As I reached the third floor hallway, I could hear her moaning. I found a woman on the floor, on her side, and holding onto her abdomen. "She doesn't look very pregnant," I thought to myself. I knelt down next to her. She was moaning loud, in obvious pain, and told me she was having a baby. I saw that she was wet and there was fluid on the tile floor under her legs. I told her, "I need to take a look." She felt uncomfortable pulling up the long shirt she was wearing that covered her crotch area, but if there was a baby coming, I needed to know. I asked her to roll over onto her back for me. As she did, she yelled even louder in pain.

I pulled down her pants, soaked in amniotic fluid, to see the baby's head coming out. The baby was crowning, and I knew this meant that birth was imminent. Its little wet head was starting to come out of her body.

I looked at this new mother, and in the calmest voice I could muster, I said, "Look at me! You're having a baby, and it's going to be OK. I've delivered a baby before, and everything is going to be just fine. When I tell you to, I want you to push for me, OK?" She was panting with every breath as she looked into my eyes. She was wide-eyed with tears rolling down her face. "Push now!" I said.

That child shot out of her so fast that I couldn't even keep a good grip on the little fella. He shot right out and slid into my hands like a hockey puck. I picked him up, still attached to his umbilical cord, and simply brushed my fingers across his mouth.

I needed him to breathe. "Breathe, kid! Breathe," I said under my breath. As soon as I opened up his mouth, he started to cry, and I had his mom roll back over onto her side. The panic of the situation continued, because I knew the placenta would soon be following the child. Mom felt better, though, at this point, as she lay exhausted on the floor trying to look down at baby and me.

I looked over to the mom, and in a soothing voice, tears then running down my face, I told her, "You have a little boy." I was completely overwhelmed with joy—a joy that I had never felt in my entire life. Nothing in life had prepared me for this moment. I had just witnessed a miracle. I brought life into the world, and I was overcome with emotion as the mom and I were smiling, crying, laughing, and crying some more. Still no paramedics, no rescue personnel, or other officers had arrived on the scene yet. It all happened so quickly. I updated dispatch:

"Baker-Twenty-eight Radio, be advised I have delivered the baby, and both mom and baby
are doing fine. Advise the ambulance we are in the laundry room on the third floor,
and I am in a holding pattern waiting for them to arrive."

I could hear cheering in the background of the dispatch center, and the amount of happiness that I felt at that moment was a life-altering event for me. It seemed like it took forever for the ambulance to arrive, but it didn't end there.

I drove to Bronson Hospital to follow up with mother and baby to make sure they were still doing fine. I had no idea that I would be signing a birth certificate. However, that's exactly what Bronson Hospital staff had me do since I had delivered the baby. Later they would award me a "Blue Stork Award"—a pin with a small blue stork carrying a baby in a blanket. I had always told myself that, while a police officer, I would want to deliver a baby. I met that goal.

My shift had come to an end after the baby incident, but the emotion was still running through my body. As I put the key into the door of my truck at Station Two, I was overcome with emotion and realized the gravity of the situation, dropped to my knees, and just wept next to my truck as I looked up into the starlit sky and thanked God for giving me the opportunity to deliver a baby.

Interesting, too, is that before I delivered the baby this had been one of the worst days of my career. I was facing a suspension and an internal transfer and questioning myself in all aspects of my future career at KDPS. Thinking that my supervisors or coworkers would be questioning my personal integrity, I felt that I was pretty much dead inside.

Then, however, God sent me to deliver this baby, and I instantly realized that there is so much more in life that is bigger than myself. I was essentially reborn, too, during this incident, and I felt great about what I had done. I realized that I would not allow an internal departmental incident affect my ability to serve and protect the public I swore to defend. I was a Kalamazoo public safety officer for God's sake, and a member of an amazing team! As I reflect on my career, I am convinced that delivering this little boy into the world was meant to be and that it was a reality check sent to me by God.

"Rescue Six and Baker Sixty-One, respond to 1200 Greenwood.
Reference a possible ten-thirty-two." (Dead body)

February 1, 2009, was the day of Super Bowl XLIII, in which the Steelers defeated the Cardinals 27 to 23 in Tampa, Florida. This football game would not be without tragedy in Kalamazoo, Michigan. For one young man, a twenty-year-old Western Michigan University student, never even made it out of bed that day to enjoy the game with his friends and roommates. Instead, he would die alone in his bed.

His roommates, however, threw the typical college-style house party, complete with all the finger food you could eat, kegs of beer, football revelers, and friendly drunken games of flippy cup and beer pong. All of this fun would come to an abrupt end, though, before the football game was even over. This house of fun and festivities would soon become a house of death and tears, ruining the night for everyone in attendance. The event would remind me for every Super Bowl Sunday to come to say a little prayer for the life of a young man who died so young.

I was greeted at the front door by two young men who seemed to be distraught. As I walked through the front door into the living room, I could smell the odor of death through the smell of spilled beer, cooked hamburger, salsa, cheese, and chips. The floor was littered with red party cups, and a piece of plywood was set up for games of beer pong on two saw horses. The mood in the house was a mix of drunken fun and the sobering effect of the reality that was quickly setting in on the roommates of the deceased who met me at the door.

I was escorted to the basement area where several rooms were established for each roommate. Through a doorway hung with curtains, I found the dead body, whose odor was becoming more pungent with each step toward the back room. In the bed I found a clothed male subject, lying with his face turned toward the wall. Rigor mortis had set in. This young man was obviously dead and beginning to rot. I verified that he had no pulse, wasn't breathing, and had lost bowel and bladder control. He had been dead for at least most of the day.

The responding rescue unit was advised to disregard. The EMS paramedics followed their dead body protocol, and the medical examiner was notified to include the local body recovery unit. The only type of medication found inside his bedroom was an asthma inhaler on the bed stand next to the body. The parents were notified in person by other officers of the death of their son, and it was determined that the victim did in fact suffer from asthma. When I followed up with the family of the victim, they told me that this was the second son who had died under age twenty-one. I later found out that an autopsy revealed the cause of death was an asthma attack. What bothers me about this death is that it could have been prevented had someone witnessed the asthma attack.

One of the last rescue calls of my career would end with a much better outcome and one that would result in the first Life Saving Award I received from the department. This victim would also suffer a near-fatal asthma attack.

—⊶⊷—

On January 12, 2011, I was dispatched to a group home for the mentally ill. The call was dispatched as an unknown type of alarm. Strange, though, was that it was only around eight in the evening, and I knew that the home was occupied by residents and staff. I also had never been dispatched to this address for this type of alarm. Per protocol, two units were dispatched to the scene.

I arrived to find the lights on with cars in the driveway and was starting to assume the call was simply a false alarm. I made my way to the entrance of the house to see a male subject lying on the floor with his face blue. The female worker was in a state of panic and standing over his body doing nothing to help, but getting in my way.

I was thinking, "Check breathing, check pulse, begin CPR." I had no medical equipment with me at the time. I knew I had to work fast if I was going to save this guy. I opened his airway by tilting his head back—no breathing. With no CPR mask, I pinched his nose and gave a breath. There was no time to run back to my car and get the CPR mask. This was life and death, and I knew time was against me. The breaths were hard to blow into his mouth. It was as if I were blowing through a narrow straw. I felt for a pulse. *Yes*! I had a carotid pulse. In between another breath, I asked the female worker, "What happened to him?"

"I don't know," she replied.

"What's his medical condition? Why is he here?"

Another worker came into the entryway with a clipboard and yelled out to me, "He has asthma!"

"Shit," I thought. That sucks, but I could save this guy; I knew I could. "What's his name?" I said.

"Jack," she replied.

He was a younger male, only twenty-nine years old. I was hell bent on not letting him die. Another breath, one thousand one, one thousand two, one thousand three, one thousand four, one thousand five, breathe!

"Sixty-one City, be advised I have a subject in respiratory arrest, possible asthma patient. He is not breathing. I'm giving rescue breaths. Dispatch rescue and EMS."

"Come on, Jack! Breathe, dammit!" I kept blowing into his mouth, counting, giving a breath, counting, giving a breath.

Another PSO came through the door. He was a new kid, and I don't even remember his name. I yelled at him to go to my car and grab my medical bag on the front seat. He hesitated, and I yelled at him, "Stop staring and go to 1161 and grab my black med bag!" I knew I was taking a risk by direct mouth-to-mouth contact, but in my mind I just said, fuck it, and did it anyway. Looking back, I should have used a barrier of some type. This could have been a thin towel, washcloth, paper towel, anything.

The vomit had not yet come from the victim, but I knew it was going to be on its way soon. He was struggling. I could see his eyes were bugging out, his arms were lifting up, and he was starting to kick with his feet. I kept yelling at him, "Jack, come on, man, just fucking breathe!" I blew in another breath. His airway was still so constricted it was hard to get in the air. I was worried my breaths were not enough. I wanted my damn pocket mask because the last thing I needed was for him to throw up in my mouth, but I didn't care. I wasn't going to let him die. Not while I had a chance, not while he was in my care, not on my watch. The new kid came through the door and gave me the entire black med bag. Success! I put my pocket mask on Jack's face, and the seal was much better. I was able to tilt his head back farther, and the breaths went in much easier.

Jack was finally starting to try to breathe on his own, but he still needed help. My voice was helping. I was telling him to breathe just before I blew more air into his lungs. His color was coming back, too, and I was feeling the life come back into him. "You're doing fine, Jack. Keep breathing. It's gonna be OK, man!" The paramedics and the KDPS Rescue Six medical first responders arrived. I wasn't moving for anyone! I quickly told the medics he was in an asthma attack and in respiratory arrest when I arrived. I kept breathing for him in between my sentences to the medics. They wasted no time in pushing the drugs and attaching a breathing treatment to a bag valve mask. Jack didn't like the air being forced into his lungs, but he had to have it. He was slowly starting to breathe more on his own, but he was like a fish out of water, still in a panic for air with his arms trying to push the bag off his face and kicking with his legs. I just kept blowing and yelling at him to calm down and to breathe with me.

The breathing treatment and drugs given by the paramedics really helped him, and he began to calm down and to finally breathe on his own. So we switched the oxygen mask over to a nonrebreather mask, and he was doing all the breathing on his own and starting to regain consciousness.

He kept tugging at the mask, though. When he pulled it off his face, he looked right into my eyes and spoke his first words: "You saved my life."

"It's OK, Jack, you're gonna be OK now. Just relax and take some slow deep breaths for me, OK?" I fucking did it! I really did save a life.

By the time Jack was loaded up on the ambulance cot, he was completely alert and breathing on his own. As we loaded him into the back of the ambulance he looked at me and gave me a thumbs-up. Wow, I was on cloud nine right then. I felt that nothing else in my life had mattered at all. What mattered was that Jack Young was alive, and I thank God for giving me the opportunity, ability, knowledge, and strength to do God's work.

As a result of this situation, the department awarded me the Life Saving Medal and Award on November 4, 2011. It had been nearly twenty-five years since I had become a police officer, and I did it, I finally made a real difference, at least in my mind anyway. I had direct intervention in a life-and-death situation. Of all of the awards I received as a Kalamazoo public safety officer, this award has special meaning to me.

Kalamazoo Public Safety
City of Kalamazoo
LIFE SAVING AWARD
Presented to

ROBERT T. CHRISTENSEN

Officer Todd Christensen
For exceptional and professional effort resulting in the preservation of life,
Kalamazoo Public Safety presents PSO Todd Christensen with the Life
Saving Award.

On January 12, 2011, PSO Christensen responded to the report of a man
down at 1207 Oakland Drive. Jack Young, 29 years old, was unresponsive and not breathing after suffering an asthma attack. Young's airway
was severely restricted. Officer Christensen immediately initiated aid and
performed rescue breathing for Mr. Young. Officer Christensen continued
to breathe for Mr. Young for approximately five minutes until paramedics arrived to assist. Approximately twenty minutes later, Young was able
to breathe on his own. Officer Christensen is commended for his life-saving
actions, exemplifying the highest standards of the Public Safety profession and
saving the life of Jack Young.

Life Saving Award presentation by Chief Jeff Hadley

HONOR GUARD: THE TEARS

BEHIND OUR GLASSES

KALAMAZOO PUBLIC SAFETY HONOR GUARD

*"Pride is a personal commitment. It is a matter of attitude
that separates excellence from mediocrity"*
William Blake

I n January of 1992, I was chosen to be part of the only specialty unit that I would remain on for my entire career. It was an honor to serve with some of the most dedicated and committed officers in my life. The honor guard officers I served with over the years held our profession in the highest position of honor possible. We had an obligation to honor not only the fallen officer, but also the family, friends, and coworkers of the fallen. Our commitment was to ensure that the proper police and military honors were endowed to the fallen and their family to leave a lasting impression of a time-honored service for the fallen officer. No other duty throughout my career would see such levels of anguish, pride, emotion, distress, and fellowship than that of a Kalamazoo honor guard officer.

Our honor guard team would receive notification via the LEIN system of any officer-involved, line-of-duty death in the state of Michigan. We would travel throughout the state representing Kalamazoo Public Safety at all in-the-line-of-duty deaths. In many cases, an agency would request that our honor guard be the primary representing honor guard to render all police funeral duties. Typically in these cases, the requesting agency didn't have an honor guard of their own and wanted to ensure the best possible police funeral for the family of the fallen.

We were well versed in casket guard detail, changing of the guard, rendering the final salute, organizing the ranks of visiting officers, providing a color guard detail, conducting the flag-folding ceremony at the graveyard, presenting the flag to the chief of police (and sometimes the family), including the final shotgun salute that replicated the military twenty-one-gun salute for the fallen, and taps. At the end of the ceremony, we made it our own tradition to present to the family the empty twelve-gauge shell casings fired during the three-round volley of fire. To enhance the effect of the shotgun blasts, we used blank round cartridges in our silver Winchester shotguns to increase the sound of the blast and the smoke upon firing. We wanted to be impressive.

Before any ceremony or funeral service, our team of officers would go through a period of scrutinizing each other using lint brushes to ensure no lint, thread, or particle was on our uniform. Each piece of equipment had to match and be highly polished. Boots were spit-shined, laces were a clean white, and badges and collar brass were fingerprint free. Absolute perfection is what we were striving for. Many times this period of self-scrutiny would also result in a barrage of constant jokes and personal attacks on each other. It helped lighten the mood of the seriousness of our situation and helped us each cope with the emotional trauma of death that surrounded the event.

We would arrive early at any event to allow time to practice each movement or technique. "Go through it again, again, and again!" our commanders would insist. A funeral must be flawless when we were on stage with an audience. First, a recon of the area to conduct the movements would be in order. This meant meeting with the funeral home directors to see where the body and flowers would be placed. We had to know if it was an open or closed casket and how long the visitation would last before the funeral would begin. Practice of the casket guard techniques and changing of the guard took place. Flag folding practice, final salute, final shotgun salute, playing of taps—all of these moving parts were practiced and practiced before the funeral would begin. Sometimes though, practice time was limited, so you had to be focused and on your A game, ready to go at any moment.

We would also meet with the family member who seemed to be organizing the event with the funeral home director. Our job was to make the funeral perfect for them. We were there for the family, and our performance must be perfect. Being perfect wasn't always that easy for me. As a night shift officer, an honor guard call-up could be happening the very next day. Yes, that meant no sleep for Officer Todd. I would take advantage of the drive to wherever we were going to get in a small nap in a car full of loud-talking, wide-awake cops who enjoyed joking around and badgering one another. I could sleep right through it all.

Our uniform consisted of a more dressed-up version of our normal class-A uniform: highly shined combat boots with white laces to match our white gloves and neck ascots, a navy blue campaign-style hat, specialty badges, unit award, nametag, and leather jacket for cold weather events. There was no rank in the honor guard. Everyone needed to look the same. Uniformity was key!

The funerals all seemed to be the same to me. The mood was a somber state of sadness for all in-the-line-of-duty deaths. We would see the masses of uniformed officers show up to file into ranks before entering the church or other large building. The other honor guard units from around the state were almost always present, and each unit lined up near the front of the church with its colors posted at the entryway. As the funeral would begin, the bagpipes would play, and the family would make its way into the church first.

"Detail, Present Arms!"
The hand salute was rendered, flags were lowered, and weapons adjusted
to a salute
as the family of the fallen made its way into the church.

Once the family members and civilians had entered the church, the rank and file of officers would follow. Entering the church, all officers, each in turn, would remove their headgear, place their hats over their hearts, and make their way past the casket of the fallen officer as pass and review was conducted. It gave each officer a moment of silence to him or herself and a chance to say goodbye to the fallen comrade. Never was a dry eye present, and faces were somber as each officer took his or her place among the ranks and then to a seat.

As I would make my way past the fallen officer I would ask, "Will I be next? Will I be the next funeral? Will they all come to see my body? What will my family do? The families of the fallen must feel so empty, so helpless. Which one of us will be the next to die?" It was a powerful reminder that our chosen profession can become deadly. However, there was a sense of calm knowing that my brothers and sisters in blue, brown, green, or Canadian red would be there to give me and my family the proper good-bye if that day ever came.

What is so wonderful about Kalamazoo Public Safety is that our honor guard performs every funeral that a family requests for our own. Past or present public safety officers are all given that final respect by the department, the city, and the community they swore to protect. Often, we would conduct funerals for retirees from years gone by. Only pictures in a church lobby or in a funeral home would be all that reminded those in attendance of the proud heritage the passing officer had lived. It was a pleasant reminder to me that, even after my retirement and into my old age, the Kalamazoo honor guard would be there to give us the final respect we earned and deserved as public safety officers of Kalamazoo. It is comforting to know my brothers in blue will see me off. I love them for that.

IT'S OK TO DIE

Do you believe in God? This is a question we all ask ourselves, I'm sure, at some point during life. How about near-death experiences? Life after death? Heaven? Hell? The supernatural, for that matter? Perhaps it could be blamed on my lack of sleep from working the night before a funeral, but I truly believe I did have an experience with the afterlife.

Officer Scott Flahive of the Grand Haven, Michigan, police department was murdered in the line of duty on December 13, 1994. The Kalamazoo honor guard attended the event, like many others from around the state, but on this day I would find myself in a situation I've only described to my family and never revealed to anyone else. At the time, I felt this moment was meant for only my eyes and my mind. It was intended for me to hold in a special place within my heart. Since that time I feel that perhaps if I shared my experience that others might find peace from it.

It was a cold December morning in 1994 when our honor guard team drove to Grand Haven to attend Scott Flahive's funeral. The day was especially cold with a cold rain and temperatures hovering just above freezing. Our team provided a color guard detail and made our way from the location of the funeral service to the graveyard where Officer Flahive would be laid to rest. As the hundreds of patrol cars found their parking spots and the bagpipes played, the ranks of officers formed at the gravesite and were all called to attention as the body of Officer Flahive was removed from the hearse. The flag-draped coffin was slowly pulled out and the commands were given.

"Detail, attention!
Present arms!"

While standing at attention and holding my salute, I was shocked at how the drizzle and rainy December day simply stood still for just a moment. I was happy the rain had finally stopped for the ceremony and was slowly being warmed by the sun that barely made its way through the parting clouds above. I remember that the sun felt so good at that moment because we were all shivering from standing outside for so long and getting completely soaked in rain. It was the type of wet-cold that goes right through you at that temperature.

Why the hell is someone laughing? As the sun warmed my face, I could hear laughter coming from the ranks to my left. I was in disbelief that someone would actually be laughing, not paying attention during such a somber moment, and completely lacking self-discipline and respect for the fallen officer. The laughing continued, and then I could see movement to my left. I was trying to look out of the corner of my left eye without moving my head to see what idiot was creating all the commotion. I finally had to do it! I slowly turned my head while maintaining my hand salute and saw not an officer out of order, but the spirit of what I believe in my heart to be that of Officer Scott Flahive. It was a being, a vision, I don't know what, but it was clear that I was having a spiritual moment. As I looked to my left I saw the body of a man dressed in a white flowing gown floating toward me and laughing. Yes! Laughing! His hair was as blond as the sun, and he floated in and among the officers who stood at attention within the ranks, passing through them and around them in a fast manner and just laughing. I saw the spirit moving in my direction, and he simply flew past me and vanished in the ranks to my right.

I thought, "Does anybody else see this?" I was looking around and nobody was reacting. The feeling that immediately followed the passing of what I believe was the spirit of Scott Flahive was an overwhelming sense of calm and happiness. I simply thought to myself, "It's OK to die." This is the only feeling I can explain. I just knew that it was OK to die. I can still see myself smiling as the spirit passed by me, and the sun warmed my face. I have no other way to explain the situation to myself, and I kept it a secret.

At first, I thought I should tell someone, but then I thought, "No, this was meant for me." But as the years passed, I felt more compelled to reveal what I had seen. I told only my mom, dad, and two sisters about this. I hope that by revealing this special moment, perhaps it will help to bring peace and calm to others. I never feared death after this moment in my life.

Officer Scott Flahive was shot and killed after he stopped a vehicle that contained two recently escaped criminals. As Officer Flahive approached the car, one of the suspects, who was lying in the back seat, shot through the door with a 30–06 rifle, striking Flahive and killing him instantly. The suspects turned themselves in, and the shooter was sentenced to multiple life sentences. The accomplices were sentenced to ten and fifteen years. Officer Flahive had been with the agency for four years and was survived by his parents and sister.

Accessed from: http://www.odmp.org/officer/755-officer-scott-anthony-flahive#ixzz2rRVGCuPs on March 6, 2014 at 1:27 p.m.

WHEN MY STUDENTS ARE KILLED, I DIE A LITTLE TOO

Our lives are filled with the good times and bad, but for me, as a police officer, my worst experiences have been the deaths of my friends on the force, and as a police academy trainer, the deaths of my students. Both of these nightmares came true for me, and I shall never forget them. The loss of my brothers rips my heart out of my chest and leaves a scar so deep nothing can ever heel it. The feeling comes back every year, on the dates of their deaths, or randomly at any time of the day or for no reason at all. It never gets easy to deal with, and the tears still continue to flow. I force myself to never forget them.

Two of my past academy students died less than a month apart and less than one year from graduating from the Kalamazoo Valley Community

College Police Academy: Owen Fisher and Scot Beyerstedt. I consider all of my students as family, my everything, my brothers, my sisters, and my children. Losing one to death is heartbreaking, especially as their trainer, their mentor, their drill sergeant. I would give my life for any of these people, just as they would for me.

You Will Never Be Forgotten

OFFICER OWEN FISHER, FLINT, MICHIGAN POLICE DEPARTMENT

Owen Fisher had graduated from the KVCC Sixty-fifth Academy and was clearly among the best in his class. Eager to join the ranks of cops around the state, Owen was hired soon after graduation by the Flint, Michigan, police department. Officer Fisher was killed in the line of duty on July 16, 2005. He had been a police officer for only four months and would become the tenth Flint police officer killed in the line of duty.

This was my first student killed in the line of duty. Many of his class-mates were at the funeral. Once the funeral was over and we were all making our way back to our patrol cars for the ride back to Kalamazoo, I spotted a group of his classmates huddled around each other. Accompanied by PSO Paul Bianco, a fellow honor guard officer and my teaching partner and fellow drill sergeant at the academy, we both knew, without saying a word, what we had to do.

Paul and I walked toward our group of past students, and we all simply embraced each other in a group hug and just let the tears flow. There is nothing we can do or say to help the pain. However, Paul and I knew we had to be strong. As our tears were wiped away, we did our best to give some words of encouragement to our students. For to them we are always their drill sergeants, a source of wisdom and strength. On this day, though, we were one, joined together by the strength of each other's presence in the graveyard. I can't remember what I told my troops, but I hope it helped give them some peace.

> Officer Owen Fisher was killed in an automobile accident when his patrol car was involved in a collision with a second patrol car during a vehicle pursuit. The collision also caused the patrol cars to collide into a house. Officers from the Flint Police Department and Michigan State Police continued the pursuit and apprehended the suspect a short time later. The suspect was convicted and sentenced to serve three to fifteen years for first-degree fleeing and eluding, second-degree fleeing and eluding, and assault with intent to do great bodily harm. Officer Fisher had served with the Flint Police Department for only four months. He was survived by his fiancée, parents, sister, and grandmother.

Accessed from: http://www.odmp.org/officer/17820-police-officer-owen-david-fisher#ixzz2qP8BXxtd on March 6, 2014 at 1:28 p.m.

Officer Owen Fisher
Photo courtesy of Owen's parents, David and Vida Fisher

You Will Never Be Forgotten

OFFICER SCOT BEYERSTEDT, MATTAWAN, MICHIGAN, POLICE DEPARTMENT

Ten days after Officer Fisher was killed, Officer Scot Beyerstedt of the Mattawan, Michigan, police department was killed in the line of duty. Yes, another student killed, dead, gone. The death of Owen was like a knife to my heart through my chest; Scot's death was a knife through my spine into the back of my heart. I felt completely dead inside. Like Owen, Scot had been a police officer for only four months and had graduated from the KVCC Academy. Within two weeks of being hired by Mattawan, he would be killed in the line of duty. Scot is the only Mattawan police officer ever killed in the line of duty. Both Owen and Scot were in the field training phase of their careers. They never had a chance to do their jobs.

Officer Scot Beyerstedt succumbed to injuries sustained when his patrol car crashed during a vehicle pursuit at approximately 9:00 p.m. He and his training officer were pursuing a vehicle after trying to stop the driver for reckless driving. The patrol car left the roadway and struck a tree as it rounded an S-curve. Both officers were transported to Bronson Methodist Hospital where Officer Beyerstedt died. He wasn't wearing his seat belt at the time of the accident. The vehicle they were pursuing fled the scene. The driver was arrested on August 8, 2005. He was convicted in Van Buren County on December 14th, 2005, of one count of fleeing and eluding resulting in death.

On January 6th, 2006, he was sentenced to five to twenty-five years in prison. Officer Beyerstedt had served as a part-time officer for the agency for only two weeks and had previously served with the Cassopolis Police Department for four months.

Accessed from: http://www.odmp.org/officer/17826-police-officer-scot-andrew-beyerstedt#ixzz2qPCO76iN on March 6, 2014 at 1:30 p.m.

Scot was killed just eight miles from where I live. There is a huge maple tree alongside the road that still stands where he crashed. On this tree is a plaque in his memory. Each July I make a trip out to this tree and hang a new American flag above his plaque. I guess I just can't let Scot go.

Officer Scot Beyerstedt
Photo courtesy of the family of Scot Beyerstedt

You Will Never Be Forgotten

THE WORST OF DAYS: "TAKE BAKER TWENTY-TWO OFF THE WATCH."

April 18, 2011, was by far the most tragic day in Kalamazoo public safety history. It was on this day that Kalamazoo lost its first officer to an in-the-line-of-duty death. Killed in the line of duty does not do him justice. PSO Eric Zapata was murdered in the line of duty! Not a student this time, but a partner. My brother, my coworker, my friend, and, yes, even one of my new kids. I was one of PSO Zapata's field training officers when he first started in Kalamazoo ten years earlier. I remember him with some of the fondest memories. In particular, Eric was full of laughter, and that laughter spilled over to everyone he met. Of the many great times we had together, I will never forget two of those moments, and I cherish them with all my heart. I have not previously shared either with many others, but now it is time to share his love of life and laughter with the world.

When Eric was hired, I thought to myself, "Great! We finally hired a Latino officer who can speak Spanish for me when I need an interpreter." Minority officers are a jewel for Kalamazoo DPS. We are fortunate in Kalamazoo to have a department that is pretty well represented by minorities and aligned very closely to the diversity of our community. For a relatively small department in a midsize American city, our agency is quite diversified in the makeup of our officers: black, white, Latino, Indian, Middle-Eastern, gay, straight, Asian. The diversity in our ranks matches the diverse make-up of our nation, helps to strengthen ethnic bonds, and promotes respect for the differences of others.

So, here was this new Latino officer, Eric Emiliano Zapata. When I told Eric how thrilled I was that we finally hired another officer who could speak Spanish, he began to laugh at me, and with his huge smile he said, "Yeah, I'm a Mexican, but I don't know any Spanish!"

"What the hell?" I said. "You can't speak Spanish?" We both about pissed our pants laughing as we pulled out of the station.

Another classic PSO Zapata moment came while we were working overtime for party patrol. I had been assigned to drive the paddy wagon around the city, pick up arrests from officers, and then transport the suspects to jail. Eric called out that he was in foot pursuit after a suspect. Shortly thereafter, as officers were responding in mass to assist him in the chase, Eric called out (out of breath) that he had caught the suspect and had him in custody. I wheeled the paddy wagon through a nearby intersection, screeched to a halt, and was the first officer to his scene.

What a sight to behold. Eric had his male suspect in handcuffs and lying face down on the sidewalk. Eric was standing over the handcuffed lad, hand on hip, with one foot on the guy's back. He was inhaling a cigarette as fast as he could and smiling as I pulled up! He looked like a scene out of a movie.

"Got him!" Eric yelled out to me, smoking and laughing. I never let Eric forget that day. It was clearly one of the funniest sites I had ever seen.

Around eleven at night on April 18, 2011, I was home in bed, off duty of course, when the phone rang. It was my best friend and the mayor of Kalamazoo, Bobby Hopewell. When I looked at my phone and saw his name, I thought to myself, "This is odd. It's a weekday. Why would Bobby be calling this late?" I answered the phone, and I could tell something was terribly wrong.

Bobby had a broken and quiet voice and he asked, "Did you hear about what happened tonight?"

I had no idea what was going on.

"There was a shooting and an officer has been killed."

"What! Who?"

"Eric Zapata was killed."

I had no words, I told Bobby in a broken voice through tears streaming down my face, "OK, thanks. Um, I'll call you later." I hung up. As I lay back in bed, memories were racing through my mind. What was I to do? I felt helpless, but there was nothing I could do. I rolled over on my side and just wept. I had to be up by five forty-five the next morning and to work by seven. Someone called me from the honor guard, and to this day I don't remember who, but they told me to report to the hospital in Lansing as soon as I got to work in the morning. I was to change into my honor guard uniform, and I was to go be with Eric's body during the autopsy. I quickly snapped myself back to reality and slept the best I could. I was up early, only three hours later, and went for a run in the early morning hours to clear my mind.

When I entered Station Two, I still had no details of the shooting. All I knew was that I had to get to the hospital in Lansing and guard Eric's body. We had a standing order that Eric wasn't to be left alone at any moment until the funeral was complete and he was buried. I walked downstairs to the locker room of the station around shift change as other officers were preparing for duty. Nobody spoke, and I shut off the radio that was playing. I was just pissed, and I wanted silence.

One other officer was changing clothes behind me and said, "I can't believe this happened. This isn't supposed to happen. They aren't really supposed to kill us."

I went off on him! "What the fuck fantasy world are you living in? It's a fucking war out there! You better get that through your goddamn head!"

Obviously, he was still in disbelief that Eric was dead. I don't feel bad for yelling at him though. I hope he realizes that it could be any of us cold and dead, fucking dead. I changed and left the station and headed to Lansing.

When I arrived at the hospital, I was directed to the morgue section, where I was confronted with a vision that is burned into my mind. There lay Eric, with only his uniform pants on, dark blue with a light blue stripe. I stopped and walked to my partner, lying on this cold metal table. My friend was gone, and I knew he was gone, but I didn't realize the magnitude of emotion that was building up inside me. I could hardly see; I felt my vision getting fuzzy as the tears welled up in my eyes. I slowly reached out to Eric and felt his cold arm. I held his arm in my hand with a tight grip. I simply stared at him as a hospital staff member walked up to me. "Just a minute, please," I said. "I need a moment." I just stared at Eric, looking at him up and down. The injury to his face, head, and chest was terrible. I cannot describe how much damage the high-powered assault rifle rounds did to his head, face, and chest. The destruction was beyond words, and I feel it would be inappropriate for me to describe the damage I witnessed.

Within a few minutes after I arrived, the autopsy of Eric's body began. I stayed away and simply sat in a chair and stared at the hospital staff as they performed the autopsy procedures. I kept my tears inside and could feel the emotion building up again. I would not allow myself to show weakness in front of the hospital staff. I needed to be strong, "KDPS strong," for Eric right then.

During an autopsy, for those who have never seen one, the body is essentially taken apart and examined. The skull is cut in half and the brain is exposed, ribs are sawn, and organs examined in detail. I would glance over only once in a while to see the procedure. To my comfort, a former coworker of mine arrived at the hospital. Julie Yunker, the director of the Police Academy at Grand Valley State University, just showed up. I always considered Julie my other sister, and seeing her was such a relief to me. Thank you, Julie girl. I love you so much! We sat and talked and tried to change the subject away from the tragedy to our times together at KDPS and at the police academy. Julie was retired from KDPS, and she has such a high level of commitment and dedication to our public safety family. Julie told me that she had heard I was going to be with Eric's body, and she didn't want me to be alone. Julie is the best!

Once the numbness of the situation had set in and my emotions were back in check I became inquisitive as to exactly how Eric had died. I only knew a few details of the situation and had no idea what really took place earlier in the night during the shootout with police. The doctor performing the autopsy explained to me that Eric was killed by the first round fired that struck him in the chest, ripped through his bulletproof vest, and impacted his heart and lungs. He told me that Eric was killed instantly, probably before he even hit the ground. Of course, my attention was drawn to the massive head wound Eric sustained. The doctor reiterated to me that Eric was already dead when the suspect fired the second round into Eric's head at close range, before turning the gun on himself and committing suicide. This gave me some comfort, as it was normal for me to think of how this situation could have been avoided, but you know it could have been any of us that night. Eric ran toward the sound of the guns to back up a fellow officer involved in a running gun battle with the suspect. Without hesitation he rushed to help his partner. I could only hope that I would have performed as heroically as Eric did had I been in that same situation. Eric was a true warrior.

The honor guard took four-hour shifts at the hospital, and PSO Matt Elzinga relieved me. The ride back to Kalamazoo is a blur. Once inside my cruiser, I could finally let my emotions run out. I cried the entire forty-five minutes back to Kalamazoo. I laughed at Eric out loud, yelled at him, screamed his name, and just remembered my brother. I was emotionally drained, and I felt empty, dead inside. I was a wreck.

My shift didn't end when I returned to Kalamazoo. I came back to meet with other honor guard members to start the coordination process for Eric's funeral.

The murder of PSO Eric Zapata was clearly our darkest days at the department. Yet we continued to do our duties, take our calls, respond to emergencies, and go about our work. Still, it wasn't as if nothing happened. Everyone was depressed and emotionally drained. I cannot speak for my coworkers, but for me I found the next two weeks to be terrible and unforgiving. However, I believe the tragedy brought our department closer together as an agency, a family, and as a community. Coordinating the funeral and sequence of events was by far our honor guard's most challenging duty. This funeral had to be perfect in every way! I feel that, in the end, we gave Eric the best final honors and respect he so gallantly deserved. It is my hope that by writing about him in this book that he will live in all us forever and will never be forgotten.

Officer Eric Zapata

Photo courtesy of Eric's mother, Connie Zapata-Bernal

<u>You Will Never Be Forgotten</u>

Officer Eric Zapata was shot and killed after responding to reports of shots fired. Another officer had also responded to the call and approached a man standing on a porch. As the officer asked the man if he had heard any shots, the man suddenly pulled out a gun and exchanged shots with the officer. The subject then ran in between two houses where he confronted Officer Zapata. More shots were exchanged, and Officer Zapata was struck in the head and chest. The man then committed suicide. Officer Zapata had served with the Kalamazoo Department of Public Safety for 10 years.

Accessed from: http://www.odmp.org/officer/20826-public-safety-officer-eric-emiliano-zapata#ixzz2qPcW4JJT on March 6, 2014 at 1:30 p.m.

"When a police officer is killed, it's not an agency that loses an officer it's an entire nation"
Chris Cosgriff, ODMP Founder

RESPECT ME

As I look back at my career with Kalamazoo Public Safety, Lawrence Police Department, and the US Army, I feel so much gratitude toward the many professional public servants I was honored to work with. Since you took the time to read this memoir, I hope you were able to take something from this book, good, bad, or indifferent, and found a place to apply it in your own life to help you become a better cop or just a better human being.

Whether you are a citizen, a current or former police officer, a veteran, an aspiring new officer either contemplating entering this noble profession or currently involved in a training program, or a recent graduate pounding the pavement seeking out that perfect job, I would like you to keep one thing in mind: Always have an open mind and be respectful of other people's differences.

Let's be honest, we are all human beings, and it's natural for everyone to have some sort of personal bias toward other people, call it bigoted, racist, or some other label. As a police officer you must be mindful and respectful of every different type of person who walks this wonderful planet of ours. You have to be completely neutral in your opinions, feelings, and beliefs in order to effectively enforce the laws and uphold the constitution. You cannot allow yourself to be anything but completely open and honest with yourself and others. You should also insist that your coworkers uphold the same values related to personal dignity and respect because anything else is simply an abuse of the power that you have been entrusted with. If you violate this code of ethics, consider yourself in violation of the oath of office you took when you raised your right hand and had that badge pinned on your chest.

In Kalamazoo I feel that our city and our department evolved over time and improved in the area of respecting other's differences, and it helped to make our agency a more respected and trusted organization.

As a police officer and soldier who happens to be gay, perhaps I'm more sensitive to the issues of personal dignity and respect, but I don't think so. This idea is merely opinion on my part. Throughout this book, I never alluded to my sexual orientation. Why not? Because it's irrelevant, just like race, color, religion, national origin, age, sex, pregnancy, citizenship, familial status, disability status, veteran status, or genetic information.

One can't deny that the criminal justice profession, like the military, is clearly a heterosexual-dominated profession. However, given that, I feel many members of our society find it necessary to blend their personal lives with their professional lives. I never felt this way and continue to feel there must be a division between the two worlds. I don't see how one's sexual preference plays any role in one's professional life. There simply is no place for it. What we need to realize, though, is that we must be able to accept people for who they are, not what they are expected to be. I never understood why so many people felt compelled to ask me if I was "out" at work. What does that mean, and why is it so intriguing?

My response to them was very candid: "I'm not in or out. I'm just me." My sexuality and personal life has no bearing at my workplace and has nothing to do with how I performed as a police officer, or as a soldier for that matter. Were there moments at work when I felt discriminated against because I am gay? Never! I'm proud to say that I was never personally attacked, intimidated, coerced, pressured, or discriminated against in my professional life. However, I might add that I never advertised myself either. I never hid or lied about who I was as a person. You must always be honest with yourself, or you are simply living a lie. I know there were people I worked with who were not fans of mine, and that's OK. I wasn't at work to gain popularity. I was there to simply do a job.

How people felt about me as person is their business, and I respect their opinions and their personal beliefs. However, when it involved an opinion about Officer Robert Todd Christensen or the soldier, Drill Sergeant Christensen, nobody, and I mean nobody, ever made a derogatory remark toward me. I never felt uncomfortable in any way. In fact, at Kalamazoo Public Safety, I felt even more comfortable being myself considering the antidiscrimination policies in place. The city prohibited such hateful behavior among city employees. Our working environment was respectful to people from every walk of life.

My point is that I don't want those who have aspirations to become police officers, firefighters, health-care providers, soldiers, or any other type of public servants to limit themselves with life opportunities or to stop chasing their career goals and dreams simply because they're different from what's perceived as "normal" or "socially acceptable." We are all just people.

In fact, many police agencies actively recruit officers who are minority, veterans, and yes, even LGBT officers. The more diverse an agency's ranks are, the better the entire organization will be, and the agency will truly represent the diversity of the communities it is sworn to protect and serve.

"But, Todd," you might say. "Didn't you have some awkward moments at work?"

You bet I did! I'll tell you how I dealt with them. In the one instance of derogatory remarks and bigoted comments about gays from my partner, I immediately confronted him. Would it have been easier to simply not say anything and just go along with the situation so as to not create confrontation? It could have been. However, would it have been the right thing to do? Absolutely not. I also saw this same type of positive behavior from one of my most respected supervisors.

The situation involved a shift lieutenant telling a joke over the briefing line, which was a speaker phone line linked to all stations. The shift commander used the line to provide the watch list of where officers are to be assigned for the duration of the shift and to give updates on other pertinent information relative to the shift such as stolen vehicles, runaways, BOLOs (notices to "be on the lookout"), officer safety concerns, or training announcements. The briefings took place at shift change twice daily.

On one particular evening, the shift lieutenant found it comical to tell an off-the-cuff joke about a person who had to take himself to the emergency room to have an object removed from his rectum. In the course of telling the joke, it was indicated that somehow this medical emergency was related to sexual orientation. Interestingly, the lieutenant telling this joke was a minority also. Of course the race of the supervisor is irrelevant, but I want you to see that race makes no difference when we are talking about hatefulness and a lack of respect to not only our fellow coworkers but also our society in general.

While we all sat at the briefing table listening to the joke I could see the look on my supervisor's face was not good. He was clearly disturbed by the event. As I looked around at my fellow officers at the table, I could also see that they were just as unimpressed.

In fact, one of my partners spoke up after the briefing line was disconnected and said to our group of officers, "Did he just really fucking say that?" I just shook my head, got up, and went out to my patrol car. I felt sick to my stomach that someone I had once respected had now lost all of my respect as a human being.

The next day when our shift started and the briefing lines rang, the same shift commander was giving the briefing and started out the briefing with an apology to the entire shift: "I just want to begin with saying that I am sorry for making the joke yesterday at briefing. I was completely out of line and it was inappropriate as I'm sure I offended some of our members, and I'm sincerely sorry."

You know, in our profession we have a saying: "Once you lose your integrity, you never get it back." Does it matter that he apologized? Not really. It's all well and good to say your sorry, but the fact of the matter is *you* said it and *you* think it. Just like a murder suspect who's being sentenced to life in prison and apologizes for committing murder. That's nice, but you're still a murderer, and you're still going to prison.

How do we, as police officers, change our negative attitudes of disrespect toward the very people we're supposed to serve and protect? This is clearly a human question we must all address.

In 2007 I was mobilized to Fort Benning, Georgia, and served as a senior drill sergeant at 2/58 Infantry. During basic training, a drill sergeant really does hear it all, and the new soldiers never cease to amaze me with some of the shit they come up with. My fellow drill sergeants know what I mean when I say each of us is a father, brother, satanic devil, god, guardian, protector, mentor, and coach who is hated, loved, and envied. Just about anything you can think of that a drill sergeant is, well that's what we are to the citizens we are transforming into soldiers.

Basic training can be emotionally and physically challenging for everyone at some point during training, but once in a while we see a soldier really lose it and snap. One such incident took place in the spring of 2008. Let's remember we were a nation at war in 2008, and my mission was to train and make battle-ready every infantry soldier whom I was honored to instruct. Most of them deployed, many survived, and some were killed. It's called war!

It never fails, though; there are some who, in the course of their training, will try to get out of their contract with America and do anything they can to be discharged and sent home. One such incident took place in my platoon.

The evening was winding down. The soldiers had eaten dinner and were in the barracks conducting remedial training and engaged in a competition to see who could disassemble, reassemble, and perform a functions check on both the M-249 Squad Automatic Weapon (SAW) and the M-240 Bravo Machine Gun. All the while, I played the *Empire Strikes Back* theme music. Before the music ended, they were to finish this battle drill. After all the teambuilding was finished, and the platoon was sent off for personal time, there was a knock on my office door.

"Enter!" I screamed out. In walks this private, head hung low, and I could see he was starting to cry without even saying a word. "Oh, great." I thought. "This little shit wants to either kill himself or he's homesick."

He stood before me, sniffling.

"What do you want, Private?" I asked.

"Drill Sergeant, I just can't take it anymore?"

"Stand up straight and lock it up when you talk to me!"

I scolded him for losing his military bearing. "Now what's wrong with you?"

The tears and sobbing started while this young private went on and on, telling me how he was homesick and afraid to go to war.

"Well, welcome to the crowd," I said. "Listen, nobody wants to go to war, Private, but sometimes we *get* to go to war. You should be honored that your country chose you to defend America. Besides, you volunteered, right?"

"Well, yes, Drill Sergeant, but—"

"But what? We're all going to war anyway, so let's just enjoy life while we can. Now what's really wrong with you?"

"Drill Sergeant, I'm just…I'm…I'm just not into it."

"Into what? The army or going to combat?"

"I just don't think I can do it."

"You don't think you can go to war and kill terrorists?" My voice started to get loud as I was trying to think about my next line in an effort to defeat his negative thought process and convince him he was part of something bigger than himself. I knew that this could be a defining moment in his life, and that it could set the stage for success or failure in his future. I knew that it could be something from his past that had gotten into his head to convince him that he should simply give up and quit.

"Drill Sergeant, my girlfriend is cheating on me, and I want to go home."

"You can't go home!" I responded.

"Well, I don't want to die!"

"Ah, ha! So she's not cheating on you then, right?"

"Well, no, I mean, Drill Sergeant, I…I just want out."

"Out of the army, Private?"

"Yeah."

"You mean, 'Yes, Drill Sergeant'!" I barked back at him.

"Yes, Drill Sergeant," he said, with his head held high, tears running down his face.

"Sorry, Private, you're staying, and you're going to fucking war with the rest of us!"

"Well then I'm gay," he said.

Keep in mind he just broke military policy, and by all rights I could have simply kicked his weak ass out of the army for violating the don't-ask-don't-tell policy for which many new soldiers had been released previously.

"Oh, really?" I said. "Hold up your right hand and point your finger in the air."

He hesitated.

"Do it!"

As he stood there with his right arm extended, hand in the air, finger pointing to the sky, I said, "Do this." I held my own finger up in the air and simulated pulling a trigger with my forefinger. The private did exactly what I was doing and bent his finger just fine.

"See, your trigger finger still works, doesn't it? I don't give a shit if you're gay or straight, you can shoot, so you're not going anywhere. Get the fuck out of my office!"

He dropped his head, turned around, and tried to walk out.

"Stop right there! Get back here and do an about-face!"

He returned to his position, locked it up to attention, executed his about-face properly, and took three steps toward the closed door.

"Hold it!" I yelled. "Private, I want you to get a piece of paper and write down everything you can think of that's bothering you, and you bring that to me in the morning, and I mean everything. Fill up both sides and use more than one. I want to know everything that's on your mind. Give that to me after breakfast."

I had to be tough on him. I could not just let him quit on himself, and I didn't want him to think he could just get out of a contract with Uncle Sam so easily. Besides that, I really wanted to know how to help him. I didn't want him to give up on himself. I couldn't give a shit about sending him off to combat. But, I wanted him to learn that he could solve a problem when faced with adversity regardless of how hard he thought life was.

This young soldier never quit, and he ended up staying in the army and graduating from basic training, infantry training, and airborne school. At graduation he thanked me for not letting him quit. Success! I don't know what happened to him after that. I just hope that a life lesson was learned regardless of whether or not he was gay or straight. As I said before, it's irrelevant. It's simply about being human.

Perhaps, too, those who have taken to heart what I took the time to say about myself and my coworkers will have a renewed understanding of what it really means to respect other people. In no way am I trying to push my beliefs on anyone. However, surely we can all agree that opening up the lines of communication and having a conversation about the issues that face our society today will only result in a better understanding of each other. Such communication will help form a sense of mutual respect and understanding toward those that are different. I mean, after all, isn't that part of what being a police officer is all about?

I'm sure that even some people who know me and are reading this book are telling themselves, "My God, I had no idea he was gay." Well, as you say this to yourself then ask this question: does it really matter? I think that we should simply realize that people come in all different types. Even if they are not stereotypical of what you perceive to be reality, it really makes no difference, right?

A wonderful person in my life once told me that your real friends are those who know all about you and are still your friends. Everyone else, well, I guess they weren't really you're friends. Throughout the course of my police and military career, it wasn't my intent to make new friends. I was there to work and my job was to be a cop or a soldier and to serve my community and my country.

EPILOGUE

Throughout this memoir, I listed only those special moments that I felt had an impact on my life as an officer and helped mold me into a professional as my career progressed through the years. There were several other moments certainly noteworthy, and many days that were just utterly boring as hell. As officers we are faced daily with life-altering and potentially life-threatening situations to both the public and ourselves. I did my very best to arrive to work early for every shift and to be completely mentally and physically prepared to face the unknown challenges that presented themselves during each shift I worked.

To begin this process of mental preparation, I would start out my day with as much sleep as I could get and begin most days with a moment of personal time by conducting a physical workout of some type. A solid hour was dedicated for me to come to a neutral place mentally and to prepare myself physically to meet the stresses of any given situation. Too many times, officers sacrifice their own health and fail to maintain their bodies in a peak physical condition. Remember that police work is a young person's game. We cops will get older each year, but the criminal element remains the same. You can't waiver with your mental and physical level of wellness. I would go to work in civilian clothes, change into my uniform at the station, and prepare mentally to be a warrior for the next twelve hours of criminal patrol. At the end of the shift, I would take off that uniform, change my clothes, and leave the stress of work at work without taking it home with me. I would leave the station as just Robert Todd Christensen.

Throughout this book I tried to capture the emotion and internal thoughts of what was going through my mind as I handled each call. The one theme that kept coming back into my thoughts, though, was that I worked with some of the most professional, compassionate, respectful, and caring people our society has to offer. At work, I laughed the most, cried the most, loved life the most, and at times, yes, hated every aspect of the job. In the end it was my fellow coworkers who really made Kalamazoo Public Safety a wonderful place to work. I am forever grateful to my friends and coworkers, the citizens, and the city of Kalamazoo for providing me with such fond memories. I hope that I helped to instill this same feeling of appreciation and gratitude to those who took the time to read this book.

During the last year of my career, I had plenty of time for reflection. I was in my final year at Public Safety and had signed my early-retirement-incentive agreement. I was thinking about how grateful I was to work for such a wonderful city and a great community. It was comforting to know that even into retirement the city would pay for my life. Not to diminish my career in any way, I mean I clearly paid for my pension with every paycheck and planned for the inevitable end, but I wasn't satisfied. I wanted to do something for the city that I protected for all of those years. I wanted to show my sincere appreciation to a department of professionals.

Then the idea came to me through the US Army. Since my deployment to Afghanistan in 2009 and 2010, we received briefings from several military organizations about the benefits of being a combat veteran. One of those briefings was from the Employer Support of the Guard and Reserve (ESGR). The Secretary of Defense Employer Support Freedom Award is the highest award given by the US government to employers for exceptional support of its employees serving in the guard or reserves. As the nation increasingly calls upon the reserve components (RC) to serve in combat zones or respond to humanitarian missions, America's employers have become inextricably linked to the nation's defense. The Department of Defense recognizes the impact this has on employers nationwide and honors the most supportive employers annually with the Secretary of Defense Employer Support Freedom Award.

Secretary of Defense William Perry authorized the first award in 1996. Employers are nominated for the Freedom Award by the guard and reserve service members they employ or their employee's families. The nominations include a detailed description of an employer's measures supporting their guard and reserve employees. A thorough selection process narrows the thousands of nominations to the final fifteen award recipients.

In April of 2012, a National Selection Board comprising senior defense department officials and business leaders, considered thirty finalists from the initial pool of 3,236 nominations. Board members evaluated employer policies, practices, and programs supporting guard and reserve employees, their families, and the military community before selecting the recipients. The fifteen selected recipients were approved by the Secretary of Defense as the 2012 Secretary of Defense Employer Support Freedom Award winners.

The Kalamazoo Department of Public Safety was selected as one of the recipients of the 2012 ESGR Freedom Award. Mission complete! On

September 20, 2012, the department was presented with the award at a ceremony in Washington, DC. I was so proud to be able to award my department for its great work. It was nice to be able to give something back to the agency. The department certainly earned this award.

Kalamazoo Department of Public Safety
Kalamazoo, Michigan

The Kalamazoo Department of Public Safety (KDPS), located in Kalamazoo, Michigan, protects the citizens of Kalamazoo. With 303 employees, the Department prefers to hire both veterans and current military members. In fact, veteran status elevates a potential employee in the hiring process. KDPS has a strong commitment to caring for its Guard and Reserve employees, complete with its own Family Support Group. When a deployed KDPS Officer was severely wounded by a grenade exploding in his right hand, KDPS flew a contingency of fellow Officers to Walter Reed National Military Medical Center to be with the Officer and support his family while they relocated to Washington D.C. for his recovery. When the service member returned to work, unable to use his right hand, the Department trained the Officer to shoot left-handed, so he could keep the same job he had before he left. Army Reserve Master Sergeant Robert Christensen nominated the employer for the Freedom Award because of the support he witnessed for his fellow military employees and the KDPS treatment of him when he was deployed, sending care packages, staying in touch on a weekly basis, and providing a special homecoming. "The Kalamazoo Department of Public Safety actively supports their Guard and Reserve employees and makes it easy for us to serve both the Department and out Nation," said Christensen.

ESGR Freedom Award presentation, Washington D.C (US Dept. of Defense photo)
Pictured from left to right: Assistant Chief Karianne Thomas, Sergeant Paul Bianco, Officer Robert T. Christensen, Kalamazoo Mayor Bobby Hopewell

I started the last day of my shift just like I had started the previous shifts. I arrived at work early and was ready to go by six thirty. I was always a half hour early and prepared for work. I pride myself on having never been late for work throughout my career, and I was never a "minute man."

This day, however, was somber. I took my time driving around the city on patrol for the last time. Dispatch was kind to me also, and they did their very best to keep me from responding as a primary officer to calls and continually placed me in a backup officer position. I thank them for that, but in reality I wasn't changing my routine. In fact, I stopped my last traffic violator just five minutes before shift change. I didn't give a ticket, of course; just a verbal warning would suffice for this citizen.

I was honored in the afternoon with our traditional retirement ceremony in the chief's office with cake, awards, refreshments, and going-away speeches by command. I did have the last word, however, and simply thanked all of my friends and coworkers for doing such a fantastic job. Retiring from the department was extremely emotional for me. As I look back I can say with an honest heart that the decisions I made along the way may not have been the perfect decisions, but they were my decisions. I always made decisions with the public's best interest in my mind. Upholding the constitution was my montage, and I hope that when others remember PSO Robert Todd Christensen that they will remember a hard-working officer who was dependable, proactive, and willing to sacrifice for his fellow officers.

As I look back at my career with Kalamazoo Public Safety I ask myself, "What did I do to help make the department a better place?" It's great to be a proactive officer, hunt down criminals, prevent crime, fight fire, save lives, enforce the law, and run down an investigation to a successful prosecution. However, what did I do that is everlasting? Did I make a real difference? I'm proud to say that I left Kalamazoo Public Safety a better department than when I started. My personal accomplishments and contribution to the department included:

- Prepared and submitted a grant application that resulted in an award to the department from the AAA of Michigan grant program for the purchase of new Jaws of Life extrication equipment.

- Developed the agency's ice rescue training program, equipment purchase, and policy creation for ice- and water-related rescue emergencies, including assisting on the project to purchase a new water rescue boat.
- Proposed and designed the first ever bike patrol uniform.
- Spent my entire career as an Explorer Post advisor for Kalamazoo Public Safety's Explorer Post 265 where I helped to mentor, train, advise, and coach many of our Explorer Scouts to advance in their careers and become public safety officers and dispatchers. Some have even excelled to become supervisors within the department. I mentioned before that the greatest honor for me within the department was that of a field training officer, but my proudest moments, of which there are many, were seeing my young Explorer Scouts become successful in the years to follow while they achieved their dreams and goals of earning the title of Kalamazoo public safety officer.

I challenge each of my colleagues to do the same thing for our department. Don't just show up to work every day. Before you know it, it will be time to retire and move on in life. Make a difference in the lives of those you work with, those future officers, and more importantly for the community you serve. Live the words that embody the City of Kalamazoo mission statement:

"Doing our best work today and every day
to make Kalamazoo the best city it can be tomorrow."

Kalamazoo Public Safety
City of Kalamazoo
Retirement Recognition Award
Presented to
PSO Todd Christensen

Kalamazoo Public Safety does hereby commend PSO Todd Christensen on the occasion of his retirement after twenty-two years of exemplary service to this department and to the citizens of Kalamazoo. During the course of his career, he served as a Patrol Officer, Field Training Officer, Background Investigator, Explorer Post Advisor, Community Policing Officer and long-standing member of both the SWAT team and Honor Guard. On multiple occasions he distinguished himself through outstanding performance and is the recipient of numerous formal commendations as well as letters of recognition from citizens whom he has served. During the course of his career, PSO Christensen received multiple departmental awards, including two Chief's Awards of Excellence, two Awards of Merit, Two Professional Excellence Awards, a Life Saving Award and two Kalamazoo City All-Star Employee Awards. His dedication to duty, illustrated by his exemplary performance resulting in the preservation of life, the apprehension of several armed felons, and for developing training programs, has earned him distinction as a highly decorated Officer. Through work ethic and leadership by example, he has been a role model for those who have been privileged to work with him. A credit to this department and to the public safety profession, Todd will truly be missed.
Chief Jeff Hadley

ROBERT T. CHRISTENSEN

CPSIA information can be obtained at www.ICGtesting.com
Printed in the USA
LVOW10s1451181214

419452LV00019B/1195/P